DECORATIVE PATTERNS
OF THE ANCIENT WORLD
FOR CRAFTSMEN

DECORATIVE PATTERNS
OF THE ANCIENT WORLD
FOR CRAFTSMEN

BY

FLINDERS PETRIE

Dover Publications, Inc., New York

This Dover edition, first published in 1974, is an unabridged republication of the work originally published, under the title *Decorative Patterns of the Ancient World*, by the British School of Archaeology in Egypt and Bernard Quaritch, London, in 1930.

International Standard Book Number: 0-486-22986-6
Library of Congress Catalog Card Number: 73-79745

Manufactured in the United States of America
Dover Publications, Inc.
180 Varick Street
New York, N. Y. 10014

DECORATIVE PATTERNS

OF THE

ANCIENT WORLD

The purpose of this collection is historical, and any interests that it may claim by racial characters or charms of form are only by the way. It stands as a first outline of an index to all the decorative imaginings of man. The subject is boundless, and to wait for completion would bar any useful result. This beginning of an arrangement of the matter will serve for sorting new material into a form in which it can be compared, registered and consulted.

The limitations of the subject in this volume are where it would trench on ground which is sufficiently known already. The course of civilizations since A.D. 1000 are so far familiar that the artistic connections would not add to our history of events; the architectural studies of capitals and mouldings are so many that they form an entire subject, well-worked, which would over-balance the general history of decoration if included here; the whole theory of interlacing (ACM) or the enormous mass of mosaics in the Roman world seldom add a new form; the many long trails of degradation of forms, human, animal, and vegetable, are usually of little value, as such subjects may equally well be adopted by any people, and simplification usually follows. Geographically this series is limited to Europe and Western Asia, with their links to other lands, but ignoring designs which are special to Siberia, China, or India.

The value of decoration, historically, is due to its having no stimulus of necessity. Where an invention is obviously needed, man will repeatedly invent on much the same lines, to meet his wants. But there is no general need fulfilled by drawing a spiral, rather than a triangle or an octopus. There is great diversity of fertility in different peoples; some abound in fresh ideas—like the Cretans or Apulians, others are limited to two or three stock devices—as the Babylonians or Chinese. The historic connections of design that can be traced, with due regard to place and period, give a strong

presumption of a real connection between the designers. This may be due to descent, which will revive a forgotten style after it has been over-laid—like Late Celtic, under Louis Quinze (see LY 96); or it may be a racial movement, like the spread of Hellenism in Asia; or by trade connections—as the Mykenaean style in Egypt, or Chinese in England; or it may be owing to the labour of captives, like the foreign motives in Roman work (see LY 66, 68; WZ 2), or the plait borders unknown at Pompeii, which appear after the Dacian war.

In selecting examples, it seems best to avoid mere intricacy of overloading a basic motive, where no additional idea is added; where such were brought in, it is better to simplify them if too elaborate, as the real motive may be hidden by irrelevant complication. We do not look for hyperboles in an index.

The material subject of a design is only incidental to the quest for motives, whether it be drawn from utility, such as basketry or netting, or from beauty as in plant forms, or from religious symbols as the cross or swastika, or from art and man's device. The scale is immaterial to the nature of the form, and only convenience of size and of detail is followed here. In selection, the earliest examples are always taken, after them the most widely spread, and variants which may be found elsewhere, also any unusually late examples. The mere repetitions of common types in a country are needless for our purpose.

The numbering is designed to allow of the largest amount of expansion without irregularity; thus between 3 and 4 can come 31 to 39.

The first entry in the reference, beneath each drawing, is that of date; if known, in years, it is stated as + for A.D. or − for B.C. If the century alone is known, the middle date is entered. When no definite date is found, a guess has been made from the general circumstances, as being better than nothing, and is marked with a query. The wider divisions are by Egyptian dynasties in Roman numerals, or by the Minoan series, or by the ages of Neolithic, Bronze, and Iron. The nearest equivalents are stated in a table, on the first page of plates.

The second entry is the name of the place, when it is recorded; if obscure, the region is quoted, as the detail can be seen in the original work.

The third entry is that of the source, extracted from over two hundred and fifty works, including many long series. The abbreviations are given in a list. Commoner publications have been preferred, as being easier for verification. Arabic numerals are those of figures, if in a single book, as a translation will retain those numbers; they denote pages, if in a serial. Roman numerals are for volumes (capitals) and plates (small).

It is needless to write obvious conclusions which are seen on looking at the classified examples. Necessary notes of new conclusions and ideas are sometimes put on the plates or, if long, are in print. A plate should explain itself as far as possible, and not be issued in the dignity of silence.

I have looked forward to doing this work for the last thirty years, and prepared for it. The selection and pencilling are on my own responsibility, and most of the inking in; some inking was done by other hands, and the shields and natural plants are mostly due to Miss Phyllis Gardner's brush work. Any spare space in a plate is left as a blank for making additions.

Those whose purpose is not historical, but artistic, will be aided by the references to the original sources which they require; the sketches here are merely an index.

I hope that every twenty years or so, supplementary plates will be issued by other workers after me, and that a flood of new connections will result from discoveries.so much needed in the Middle East. This corpus is a preparation for the co-ordinating of all the new material.

NOTES.

Pls. I-III. *Hero subduing Animals.* The general idea of the A class is that of a controlling deity, which dominates the strongest powers of Nature, represented by lions, bulls, or horses. This symbolism originated in Elam or Iraq, and thence penetrated westward, mainly through Assyrian influence. The Gilgamesh series, AD, is a special form of this idea, but was linked with the rest. The female type is Ishtar, AN, passing into Astarte, AR, mixed with the Mother type of Cybele, AP 8, and the Earth goddess, AP 3, 6. In the West this passes into a deity dominating wolves, AU, or birds, AV, the most intractable creatures.

Pl. IV. *Animals.* The type of two sphinxes, or animals, with a middle column seems to start from Greece, and was continued late there, BA 8. With a middle tree it begins in Egypt, F 1, under Elamite influence; it is early in Iraq, BF 2; from Asia it came into Egypt, BC 8. Pairs of lions without a pillar appear early in Elam, BJ; and sphinxes in the West, BG.

Pl. V. *Animals.* The two snake-headed monsters, BK 2, 4, certainly passed from Sumer to Egypt. The dugong, BM 3, was the figure of Ea the god of wisdom, who rose from the Persian Gulf; it was corrupted in Assyria, as BM 5; thence it passed, under Assyrian influence in the north, to Denmark, M 8. The Glutton head, BN 2, is the main figure in Chinese decoration, where it degraded until formalised as N 4. The twisted snakes type is earliest in Egypt, BP 2, 3, but strangely survives along with rosettes in India, P 5. The form of about 2000 B.C., P 1, has a central staff which brings it nearer to the Caduceus. The two swords with guarded grips are the earliest that we know, P 1.

Pl. VI. *Vase and Animals.* This type originated in a Bacchic group, BT 2, with it a vase and plant became associated, V 2 to 5. Next a vase of fruit appears with birds of any kind, W 2, 4. The peacock was placed in decoration in China before this age, W 3, and first appears in western sculpture, on the porphyry sarcophagus of

Constantia, A.D. 330. At 560 it became usually placed with the vase and plant.

Pl. VII. *Animal Forms*. The triskele appears first about —1500, CB 12; this plain geometrical form, CB 60-75, precedes the development as human legs, CD. A Roman version was the development as dragons' heads, CF. The Chinese dragon seems to be copied from a bird, about —1000, CH 2; it passed under Norse influence, CH 6 (see MQ 3, 6, 84), and became denaturalised, CH 8. The Nautilus passed through various stages since —1800, CN 2. The shell is reduced, the arms formal, by —1300. Later the shell was the main object, with three arms, CO 2, and came down to —500, CO 7. Various other marine animals are difficult to identify.

Pl. VIII. *Octopus*. The naturalistic type, CR 2, of —1800 became regularised by —1600, CR 3, and formal soon after, CR 5. The eight-armed form was revived in the Dipylon ware, CR 8, and seems to have penetrated to the back of China, CR 9, where it is less likely to have been re-invented from the coast. The four-armed type soon arose, about —1400, CT 2, 4, 5. Then the two-armed which lasted to —1300. The period of transfer of the type abroad is thus indicated by the stage of simplifying: to Spain by —1500, to Brittany by perhaps —1200, CU 9. Other forms are of doubtful origin, CX.

Pl. IX. *Naturalistic Plants*. Plant forms are the earliest types of decoration, in France, DM 1, 2, and in Egypt, DM 30-66, at the beginning of prehistoric art. As no magic powers can be supposed to be gained by this variety of species, they warn us against seeing magic intent in the frequent forms of animals; the taste for beauty will produce one as well as the other.

Pl. X. *Lotus*. The lotus was but little varied in Egypt, and it spread mostly from the Assyrian form, DR 4; from this it entered Cyprus and the West, also passing into Scythia, DR 9.

Pls. XI, XII. *Lily*. The lily was adopted in Crete about —2000; EA 2, 5. It became formalised by —1400, EC 3 (see FH 1, 2), and lost to nature, EC 7. In Syria it passed to a different type, BC 8, which was fully treated, as a botanical exposition at Amarna, in —1370. There the parts were clearly set out, ED 2, the pistils (marked P), the anthers (A), the calyx (C), and the spathe with a withered tip (S). These parts continued to be distinguished when the form was borrowed in other lands, down to the Hittite form, EK 7. At this stage it underwent a formalising by the Assyrians,

who did not understand it, EM 3, which may be called the bowl type. This went through western stages till it became ES 4, 5, 6, and then grew into a third form, ET 2, 3. Then this ran through a thousand years of classical varieties until it disappeared as EY 7, 8, 9. A detailed account of the development was issued in *Ancient Egypt*, 1929, p. 65.

Pl. XIII. *Palmetto*. The palmetto was brought into Egypt by 2800 B.C., FA 1, and *Emblems* 20, pl. LXXXV. It was greatly developed in Assyria, inserted in volute capitals, FB 2, 4, 5, 6, and adapted to running borders, FC. The Greek types combine the acanthus leaf, FD, with the lotus standing on a degraded form of the lily, FD 5, three subjects in one. Pl. XV. *Formal Flowers*. The fleur-de-lis form is in Japan, FG 3, almost as early as among the Franks, see QK 4. It did not enter Italy in decoration till the Papal Alliance with the Franks against the Lombards in +776, and probably vanished from architecture after Charlemagne. The development of the lily with curled and spiral petals, FH 1, 2, is important for dating this form to 1500 B.C., when it was removed on the way to Britain, 23, 56. Pl. XVIII. The foliage forms seem to pass from acanthus to wild geranium in FU 3, 4. The development of foliage, FV 6, 7, in +800, was growing into a skirl in +750, FV 1, and +825, FV 3, and became disconnected from the branch by +840, FV 8.

Pl. XIX. *Arabesques*. These start in —300, developing a bract at the fork of a branch, GB 12, into a calix form, GB 16, 2. In the Praetextatus catacomb, +180, there was a real reversion to Nature, unique in such work, GB 4, 5. The arabesque became standardised for all apse mosaics of the IV-XII centuries. The Dacian form in GB 9 may have started the Chinese Han type, GC 3 to 8. Pl. XX. *Syrian*. Another strong design was the Syrian vine border, GE 2, 3, which grew into the fine school of the IInd century, GE 7, 8. This was taken up by Rome, GE 5, where it is found by A.D. 130, and passed thus in the Ist century to the Lower Rhine, GE 4, 6. There naturalised, it was carried by the Anglian invasion into England, and it is found upon the Northumbrian crosses, GG 2, 3, 4. The strength of the northern connection appears by the type of the natural interlacing of +750, as seen at Otley, being copied unnaturally in Russia by +1234. With this design in use on the Lower Rhine, there is no need to look to Syrian monks as bringing it to the Anglians.

Pl. XXI. *Symmetric*. The translation of formal plant design, GJ 3, 4, to Persia, GJ 5, and China, GJ 6, is probably due to Roman influence. But the Han style, GK 5, must be due to Assyro-Persian influence earlier, as in GK 4, which entered Russia. Pl. XXII. *Foliage Borders*. For the Persian affinity of the Moselle work, GQ 6, and pl. LXXXVI, 70, 83, and LN 71, 75, see Notes LXXXVI.

Pl. XXV. *Rosettes*. The pattern on this Pompeian potter's stamp, HC 2, so closely resembled the Egyptian rosette, HC 3, as to suggest that a piece of old Egyptian design had been brought over in a grain ship to Puteoli, and copied.

Pl. XXVII. *Inanimate*. The hills with plants and flowers, JB 1-7, are an interesting development of scenery in 1400 B.C. The radiate pattern, JE 6, is an extraordinary union of 7 and 13 points. Pl. XXVIII. *Radiate*. The most glorious radiate form is the sun on JQ 6, a yellow disc, with red centre, shining yellow rays and spangles of light on a blue ground.

Pl. XXIX. *Spirals*. The spiral begins before the Neolithic age in the Pyrenees, at the Azilian period, LA 8, LB 6, 10. Perhaps of the same age is that in Egypt of the prehistoric (Amratian) period, LA 13, which suggests a coil of thorny climbing plant, see LXXXV, 32, 33. On the neolithic Danubian pottery, the crossing bands on the spiral suggest that it represented a bundle of grass stems, tied at intervals to make it stiff for construction, LA 26, 28. In either case, it was of flexible vegetable origin, before it became formalised. The full grasp of it was in the aenolithic, with the noble types, LA 58, 63. The S spiral was as early as the whorl, LB 6, 10. Pl. XXX. *The Looped S S* is also aenolithic, LC 16, 18, 20.

Pl. XXXI. *S Continuous*. The multiple band was favoured in Russia and Scandinavia, LC 60, 68, 70, 74, 94, 95, 96: while the spotted band belongs to the south, LC 62, 64, 66; LM 2. In Egypt, the circular spiral, C 86, 87, is of the XI and early XII dynasty, the oval, C 88, 89, is later in the XII, but was started in Ur at an earlier date, LJ 5; it was secondary in Egypt. The S with two sprigs, LD 14, or flowers, D 41, 28, 49, 56, began in —2500, and extended to —1500, LD 56. It was carried west and modified at New Grange, dated on the Irish side between —2000 and —1500. This accords with the Cretan dating. Pl. XXXII. *Band*. The band winding round centres, LE 3, similarly passed to the west and reached Denmark, LE 7, 9, in the same age,

LM 11. Pl. XXXIV. *The C Spiral* begins with LM 19, and seems to rise later than the S form. It is the earliest in Egyptian history, or M 7, about —3400. Pl. XXXVII. *Late Forms*. Spirals became fragmentary in Scythia and the north, LQ. A peculiar decoration with parallel lines of curve, LR, spread from south Russia, just reached Mykenae about 1600, but was otherwise all northern, and spread to China. R 9 and 95 are examples of false spirals, merely circles.

Pls. XXXVIII, XXXIX. *British*. The C spiral was settled in the British Isles, and the form of it, united with the lily with curved petals (extracted at the side of LS 56), comes from the flower, FH 1, 2, of —1500. The trumpet spiral was started in Crete, LV 4, about —1500 or earlier; it had passed to Britain by about +100, LX 4, and was eagerly developed later in Britain, LX 5, 7, and Ireland, LX 8, 9. The use in Britain was long before the period of Irish missions, and its arrival must have been in the Bronze Age, before it vanished from the south, probably about —1500 when other spiral patterns were transmitted. These spirals were here a thousand years before the Celts, who adopted what they found here already. The inflated style, LW, may be due to Celtic taste in each case, as it does not appear before that people. How usual spirals were for common purposes is seen in LX 98, 99, on objects in use.

Pl. XL. *Spiral Blobs*. The blob form, LY belongs to the North, a later growth of the bulbous, LV, and inflated, LW. It entirely disappeared after the Roman age, but revived by racial taste under Louis Quinze, LY 96, and infected the jewellery and furniture of that time. It appears on Roman lamps, Y 67, 68, probably due to the employment of the Gaulish captives of Caesar in the Roman potteries. The joining of spirals with a circle (often with double centres) in Britain is pre-Roman, LZ; then of Roman age in LX 4, and it continued into the Lindisfarne work, LX 5.

Pl. XLVI. *Interlacing Designs* belong originally to Norway, MN 2, 3; thence they were brought by the Anglian invasion into north England, N 4, 5, 54, 6, 66. They do not appear in Ireland till a later date, and they have no relation to the Celts, as plaits enter the British Isles a thousand years later than the Celts. Similar angular interlacing, as in rush work, entered Italy with the Lombards, and not earlier (MN 7, 73, 76, 79). It was combined with circular curves, partly by +700, MN 54, and completely by +825, MO 2. From Milan, O 4, +880, it passed to Ireland +924. It continued in more complex forms in Italy till +1132, MO 8. It is distinguished from interlacing of the Goths, for that was not angular, but curved, as in osier work, see MH 65, 68, 69. The origin of all such interlacing is probably for the screens used to subdivide tents.

Pl. XLVII. *Animal Interlacing*. Interlacing was elaborated by the Norse with animal figures and dragons, MP. The complex dragon plaiting, MQ 8 (one animal shaded to show the form), gave rise to a figure of 8 pattern, MQ 84. Wire work was developed in the north, MU 2 to 5, by +680, and copied after the Norse invasion of Ireland, MU 7, B, of +850 onward. Wire threading on a chain was also imitated, MR 4.

Pl. L. The divisions of a circle are by 4 in Egypt and early Crete, where compass-struck patterns were unknown; but by 6 in Assyria, Syria, Greece and Italy, owing to facility of division by compasses. Pls. LI, LII. *The Skirl* seems to be intended to indicate circular motion, as in PT 9, the drawing of a chariot wheel.

Pls. LIII, LIV. *Shields*. The shields of northern races yield much of the decoration which has otherwise all perished in their woodwork. The Daci, on the column of Trajan, used vegetative forms, QC, D, and the crescent QE. Torques were worn by Daci, QF, and by Celts, QG; one was on the left arm, as in the story of Tarpeia, and two or four for higher ranks. On the column of Aurelius, the enemy in chain armour were the Marcomanni, as such armour was used in Holstein, QH. The Quadi used scale armour of horn (Ammianus), and this identifies the type, QK 1. The fleur-de-lis, K 4, is probably of the Franci, who were in the war of A.D. 417. The shields, QR 2, 3, 4, may be of Roman legions. The circular shield belonged to Greece and Gaul, QT, V. The Scythian type is identified by QX 2, but became so fashionable in art, that it is hard to draw conclusions from its presence in Gaul, X 5, and Etruria, X 6, 7. For the signs on Scottish gravestones, which appear to be shields and broken spears, see Pl. LXXXVII: as this origin has not yet been discussed, they are left in the miscellaneous class.

Pl. LV. *Band of Balls*. This pattern seems poor as a design, but it was very popular in the north. It touched the south at Mykenae, RN 4, and north Italy under the Lombards, RP 84, Q 4, RR 1, 2, 4, 5, 6, but never rooted there. It entered England, Q 2, 3, with the Jutes, and is found rarely on early fonts. Pl. LVI. *Architecture*. A

surprising feature, which has been overlooked, is the early use of the arch. In the neolithic age in Germany there were pillars and arches, RX 2, apparently of brickwork, with stone capitals. In Cappadocia very early arches are figured, RX 3; and in Mykenae by —1700 there were actually pointed arches, RX 4. After these, it seems likely that the later figures, X 5, 6, 7 were also of arched buildings. The spiral column, which was early in Mykenae, BC 6, was in Italy by —500, RY 3, and in India by +200, Y 5.

Pl. LVII. *The Cross* was an early emblem, in Susa by about —3000, and in India, SA 4, distinguished by a double border, SA 1 to 4. This gives reason for regarding the sign in Egypt at the same time, A 6, 7, as being an emblem, and not merely a mechanical piece of line-work. It was equally known between these two countries, in Cilicia and Aleppo, A 8, 9. The more ornate barred ends, B 5 were added not later than —2000. The sign is also bordered in Egypt, C 7, and Melos, C 8. By —2600 the cross began to be elaborated in Crete, SD, and D 2 is an astonishingly early example, not far from the primitive figure, A 2. It fell into a coarser treatment on the mainland, SE. This pure equilateral form, without any ornament, SF 4, was that in the shrine at Knossos, dating about 2300 B.C., and is exactly the same as the well-known Greek cross of Christian times. It was also used in the north, by the example F 3, from Laibach. It was adapted to woven stuff for clothing, SF 7, 8, and by —1400 in a fanciful form, G 7, 8, it was probably made in Crete, and imported to Egypt for hangings. After that, it became degraded, SJ. In Assyria, SK 5 to 9, the terminals were emphasized, and copied thus in the north, SK 2.

Pl. LIX. *Christian Age*. On reaching Christian times, it is clear that the pagan forms were retained, M 3 continued as N 1, 12; M 1, continued as N 15; N 4 continued as N 45. None of the pagan ornate forms were used religiously till the Vth century, A.D. (O9,O97). Pl. LX. In the Christian monuments, the XP monogram begins in +331, and lasts till +470. The variant with the P made with Horus' lock of hair, begins +440, and continued to +560, but is common in Egypt later. The plain figure of the cross first appears in +380, and the jewelled cross in +425. The expanded terminals begin about +450. The Arian cross has discs at the terminals, SX 1, 12. The adored cross at Palenque, in Central America, has terminals of the type of +600. Such a cross may well have been taken by the Nestorian mission in +638 to China, and within the next five centuries there may have been Chinese communication with America.

A very important movement was the reforming activity of Leo the Isaurian, who tried to bring the Byzantine empire and law into a more modern condition. Part of the change was the iconoclast movement in A.D. 730, to which we must ascribe the removal of the arms from the great crosses at Constantinople, on the west doors of Hagia Sofia; and this reformation was reflected in 820, when the Archbishop of Turin abolished crosses and images in his diocese. To the same movement is due the erasure of the cross arms at the church of S. Prassede in Rome, SY 6. In 830 the cross received the addition of a second bar higher up; this short cross-piece may have represented the label, INRI, SZ 2, 6.

Pl. LXIII. *Triangle.* Among triangles should be noticed the peculiar half rhombs, TR 7, 8, 9. On the last named the circles contain two small circles, as in late Celtic work elsewhere, LX 1, 4, 5; Z 4, 5, 6. Some meaning may have been attached to the sign. The curious type of the triangle with a disc on the point is as early as —1100 (TS 1), and appears again at —400 (TS 56). The main example of it on the tomb of Theodoric, TS 6, is too late in date to give a clue to understanding it. Rhombs subdivided were the favourite type about —600 (TZ).

Pl. LXVI. *Textiles.* Among weaving patterns, there is a large variety copied in the brickwork of mediaeval Iraq, UP. The reason for this is that matting is often placed over mud brick walls to preserve them from weather, and so the patterns of matting were naturally associated with such building. The net-work patterns, UN, in Britain are copied from the string nets in which pots were carried, as they were in Egypt. Hanging drapery, UR, was often in use on walls, and is one of the commonest painted subjects. The great example of imitation is in the marble stripes lining the cathedral of Monreale, marked out by the red borders of each width represented, and striped marble was selected for the apse, which simulated hangings.

Pls. LXIX, LXX. *The Swastika* is more commonly pointing backward (V; E, F, G), than forward (V; A, B). The groups here are of the simple form, then with one extra bend, and others up to 5 bends. Each group is arranged geographically from west to east, to show the distribution. The eastern is the earlier source. On the Indian form, see *Ancient Egypt*, 1922, 56.

Pl. LXXI. *Grooves and Steps.* The origin of the " strigil " pattern, WB 6, on Roman sarcophagi is traced back here to wide fluting, W, A and B. The step pattern, W, G to K, is purely northern, and only touches the Mediterranean at one corner. It is very persistent, and is now in general use from Scotland to China. It took possession of the gold and garnet work, which originally (WJ 2), was free from it, and ruled all the Jutish and Saxon jewellery work in England, WK 2, 3. Pls. LXXIII-IV. *Mosaics* are classed by the obliquity of the angles formed, 1:1 up to 1:3. The long hexagon embroidery in Assyria, Z 6, is evidently derived from two hexagons, one above the other, as in Z 5. The Solomon's Seal pattern, WZ 2 was probably due to Jewish captives employed.

Pl. LXXV. *Key.* The simple key patterns abound in Italy, the more interesting are the reciprocal forms, where the inter-spaces are of the same form as the solid between them, as in XA 8, and XD. The maze pattern XE 2 is the oldest known. XE 6 is not perfect, as the upper left-hand quarter does not open. Pl. LXXX. *Squares.* The expanded cross of Hartlepool, YN 7, is derived from the Ravenna type, N 5, and that obviously came from an Etruscan origin, N 4. Pl. LXXXII. The curious pattern YW 5 seems to have been copied from a grating above a doorway. The squares of varied content, YY and YZ, show what the Celt did before he acquired the spiral or interlaced forms.

Pl. LXXXIII. *The Metopic* series, ZA to E, was developed to separate squares of design around vases. In this form it precedes by a thousand years the architectural use of parallel lines between metopic groups. There is no meaning in grooving the ends of the roof beams in a building; but when that device of parallel lines to separate groups was well fixed in vase painting, it naturally was transferred to a similar duty in architecture.

Pl. LXXXV. *Emblems.* Over the head of Hittite deities is placed the sign 10 A, B, C, 11, which is recognised as the sign of divinity. It may represent a double shrine of the Mother and Son deities. A modification of this, 12, is placed beneath each of five divine figures, on a gold ring from Tiryns. The same is developed as 15 at Knossos, and this passed on to the types 16, 18 and 19; the last-named still retains the double bar of 10 A to C. Whether the Cretans recognised the original sense is quite unknown; apparently, it is merely used as ornament. Another emblem is that of the Hittite royal mark, which is found on pottery and elsewhere, 21-2-3. It appears as an amulet at Amarna, 27; also as a mould for making such amulets, No. 28; this suggests that the Egyptians traded pendants or amulets with the Hittites. A gold amulet of this type is also known, Z 9.

On the dress of the Kefti people, about the north-east of the Mediterranean, in 1600 B.C., there is placed an emblem, 36; this belonged to a previous age, as examples occur in Egypt at 2700 B.C., 32, 33; we cannot say from where they were introduced. In Asia it passed to Kashgar (37), to a reliquary of Persian (?) sources (38), and up to Lithuania, 39.

Pl. LXXXVI. Some groups are hardly assignable to any of the main classes. Fresh connections may appear in future. The wave group, 61-69, links on to some in the spiral group, LP 37, 56, of the same period and regions: but the wave forms could not all go among spirals; in order to separate these classes, far earlier examples would be needed. The strange divergent droops, 70 to 79, are un-explained: in 75 they seem to show a structure which recalls Persian or Central Asian design. The Persian affinity of 70 and 83 is puzzling in the Franco-German region; the rest of the group is in GQ 6, 7, and LN 71. In 83 the flower at the top, the droops on each side, the two commas below, and the droops at the base, are all of the fashion of Persian work, as on the dress of Khusrau, 84. Was it due to a stray party from Xerxes' expedition at 480 B.C., lost in Thrace, and pushing west to the Rhine? Their superior civilisation might well take a lead in that region. In Hagia Sofia, 85, the middle figure is almost Turkish, and is duplicated in the very foreign group in Britain, 82. Below in group 91 to 95 is the series of boss designs from China; this is an Asiatic idea which crops up in the large oval boss from the Caucasus, WJ 8, and in Asiatic-Gothic elsewhere.

Pl. LXXXVII. The Scottish emblems on tomb-stones have been supposed to represent a fibula and pin; but no pin could have a widening at each end, nor be bent. It seems rather that the group represents some form of shield reversed, and the broken spear, of a warrior. Such a long, round-ended, shield as QZ 3, 4 appears QP 4, 6, and accords with the style of Celtic shields, as seen in the example from the Thames, QZ, 46. The lunate form, QZ 6 may be the Scythian shield, QX, QY; the deeper form QZ 5 is parallel to the deeper forms QX 8, 9. The squared forms QZ 66-77 may be a square basket-work breastplate,

like the square front and back pieces on Gaulish figures at Marseilles. In the sides are circular hollows to allow freedom for the arms and, below, it descends in two cuisses over the thighs. The spear points remain in Z 2, 3, 6, 62, 64, 66. The whole idea seems to have been originally the reversing of the shield, laid longways or upside down, and the breaking of the spear, like the heralds breaking their wands at a funeral, as symbols of the end of the career. On one stone a helmet is also figured, see ACM 99. This custom would have arisen in the Bronze Age, and in the post-Christian period of these monuments the originals were probably forgotten, more or less, and the forms were confused. It may be mentioned that the animal on these tombstones, sometimes called an elephant, is probably a walrus.

Pl. LXXXVIII contains mysterious forms which may some day find a place in the series when we have much more material before us.

To sum up some of the results that we can already gain from this study: there is the great influence of Assyria on the North, in Hungary (SK 2, 5) on the Lower Dnieper (DR 9, FA 9, GK 4, 5), and extending to Denmark (BM 8); there is the movement at 1500 B.C. from Crete and Mykenae to Britain, which was probably by the Atlantic, and not from Northern lands where such designs are unknown (FH 1=LS 56, LD 56=LD 97, LE 3=LE 7, 9, LN 63=LN 67, CU 3=CU 9); there is the Syrian vine copied on the Lower Rhine, and thence brought to Northumbria by the Anglians; there is the interlaced work coming from Norway, brought by the Anglians to England, and by the Danes to Ireland; there is the Han style in China due to Assyro-Persian work; there is the Hittite divine emblem planted in Crete, and the royal emblem in Egypt; and there is the rise of arched brickwork in neolithic Germany, in Cappadocia, and with pointed arches in Mykenae. Lastly, there is a strong evidence of a wandering body from the army of Xerxes reaching the Lower Rhine.

These are some of the more definite conclusions which may already be drawn from a study of these decorative patterns; when more material is available one may expect to find many more links in the earlier ages. From these we shall view the past as a network of civilisations, peculiar to each land, and interacting on each other. We may then dis-criminate the original source of each of the devices which belonged to different areas before they were spread by intercourse.

ABBREVIATIONS.

A	Archaeologia	53
AA	Archiv für Anthrop.	1
AAF	Aspelin, Antiq. Nord. Finn	9
AAS	Aberg, Anglo-Saxons	20
ABA	Abercromby, Bronze Age	25
ABS	Ann. Brit. Sch. Athens	55
ACA	Andrae, Ceramics of Ashur	3
ACM	R. Allen, Early Christian Mons.	8
ACWA	Ayrton, C. and W., Abydos 1904	1
A-E	Ancient Egypt	61
AFW	Aberg, Franken, West-Goten	25
AGL	Aberg, Goten, Langobarden	23
AGO	Armstrong, Gold Ornaments	1
AJA	American Jour. Archaeology	8
AM	Athenische Mittheilungen	4
AN	L'Anthropologie	5
ANT.R	Antiquarium, Rome	2
AO	Alt Orient	1
AS	Andrae-Schäfer	1
AV	Arne, Necropole Vendel	12
AZ	Arch. Zeitung, Berlin	8
BAB	Boye, Age Bronze, Danemarc	2
BAE	Baldwin Brown, Arts Early England	16
BAK	Bossert, Alt Kreta	12
BAMI	Burgess, Anc. Mons., India	2
BAS	Blavignac, Archit. Sacrée	16
BAZ	Bull. Soc. Scien. Azerbijan	3
BC	Bertrand & Reinach, Celtes du Po	42
BCA	Boerschmann, Chines. Archit.	9
BEO	Brønsted, Early English Ornament	16
BGG	Bulleid & Gray, Glastonbury	28
BHG	Boyd & Hawes, Gournia	4
BIS	Banks, Bismiya	1
BK	Blegen, Korakou	15
BL	Brunton, Lahun I	1
BLM	Blackman, Meir	1
BM	British Museum	5
BMB	Boston Mus., Bulletin	2
BMCE	Brit. Mus. Cat., Early Iron Age	15
BME	Bliss-Macalister, Excavations	1

BMJ	Brit. Mus. Cat., Jewellery	1
BN	Botta, Ninève	4
BNS	Butler, North Syria	6
BP	Briggs, Pompeian Decoration	4
BQB	Brunton, Qau and Badari	3
BRG	Babelon, Monnaies Répub., Rome	3
BSA	Butler, Syrian Anc. Architecture	13
BU	Bell, Ukhaidir	4
BZ	Blegen, Zygouries	5
CA	Childe, G., Aryans	6
CAB	Chantré, Age du Bronze	1
CAC	Chifletius Anastasis Childerici	2
CAF	Chantré, Prem. Age du Fer	8
CAI	Cattaneo, Archit. in Italy	4
CAO	Contenau, Archéol. Orientale	1
CB	Carabellesi, Bari	1
CC	Chantré, Caucase, I, II, III	18
CCO	Crawford, Carved Ornament, Irish	43
CD	Childe, Dawn Europ. Civilization	23
CDA	Capart, Débuts de l'Art, Egypte	2
CDURA	Cumont, Doura	1
CDP	Childe, Danube in Prehistory	13
CIP	Cohn, Indisches Plastik	8
CMC	Chantré, Miss. Cappadoce	2
CNG	Coffey, New Grange	6
CT	Cichorius, Traianus Säule	7
DA	Ducate, Arte	5
DCD	Delbrueck, Consular Diptychen	12
DCL	Delaporte, Cylindres, Louvre	33
DCO	Delaporte, Cylindres Orientaux	3
DCP	Dussaud, Civil. Préhelléniques	8
DECA	Dalton, Early Christian Art	3
DF	Déchellete, Age du Fer	16
DF2	Déchellete, Second Age du Fer	26
DP	Délégation en Perse	5
EDE	Engelhardt, Denmark, Early Iron Age	4
EG	Espérandieu, Gaule Romaine	60
EH	Engelbach, Harageh	1
EM	Ernest Mackay, correspondence	14
EN	Excavaciones Numancia, 1912	13

PAH	Pottier, Art Hittite	1
PAT	Petrie, Athribis	1
PBS	,, Buttons and Scarabs	20
PC	Perrot & Chipiez	3
PD	Petrie, Defenneh (in Tanis, II)	10
PDN	,, Dendereh	1
PE	,, Ehnasya	1
PG	,, Gerar	13
PGR	,, Gizeh and Rifeh	2
PHBA	,, Hawara, Biahmu, Arsinoe	1
PIK	,, Illahun, Kahun	11
PKG	,, Kahun, Gurob	1
PKP	,, Koptos	1
PM	Petersen & Domazewski, Marcus-Säule	15
PMH	Petrie & Mackay, Heliopolis	1
PN	Place, Ninève	1
PNB	Petrie, Naqada & Ballas	1
PNK	,, Naukratis I	10
PO	Poulsen, Orient frühgriech. Kunst	2
PP	,, Etruscan Tomb Paintings	8
PPA	Parkyn, Prehistoric Art	1
PPE	Petrie, Prehistoric Egypt	11
PQ	,, Qau (Antaeopolis)	9
PRE	,, Roman Ehnasya	1
PRS	Porter, Romanesque Sculpture	1
PRT	Petrie, Royal Tombs, I, II	2
PS	,, Sedment, I, II	6
PSC	,, Scarabs and Cylinders	1
PSCL	Pinza, Storia Civiltà Latina	2
PTC	Petrie, Tombs of Courtiers	4
PWM	,, & Wainwright, Meydum	2
QGH	Quibell & Green, Hierakonpolis	2
R, RAL	Rivoira, Archit. Lombarda	23
RAN	Rygh, Antiquités Norvégiennes	17
RAR	Reports, Arch. Research, Kyoto	5
RCA	Romilly Allen, Celtic Art	4
RI	see RMI	
RIG	Rostovtzeff, Iranians & Greeks	9
RK	,, Kertch (Russian)	1
RMA	Randall MacIver, El Amrah	1
RME	,, ,, Etruscans	5
RMI	,, ,, Iron Age in Italy	42
RMP	Renan, Mission en Phénicie	3
RMV	Randall MacIver, Villanovans	10
RS	Riegl, Spät-römische Kunst	14
RV	Reallexicon Vorgeschichte	38
SA	Strzygowski, Altai-Iran	11
SAA	Ann. Scuola Arch. di Atena	28
SAC	Shima, Anc. Chinese Mirrors	25
SAE	Schuckhardt, Alt-Europa	3
SAK	Scheltama, Alt-nordische Kunst	9
SAYCE	(correspondence)	2
SB	Schultz & Winnafeld, Baalbek	4
SBC	Salzenberg, Bau. Constantinopel	3
SCV	Sumitomo Collection of Vases	19
SCM	Schliemann, Mykenae	1
SGLC	Segalen & Gilbert, Miss. Chine	3
SHAC	Siren, Hist. Arts Anciens Chine	2
SHET	Sarre & Herzfeld, Euphrat & Tigris	8
SHIR	Sarre & Herzfeld, Iranische Reliefs	2
SI	Schliemann, Ilios	6
SKA	Sarre, Reise in Klein-Asien	2
SM	Seager, Mochlos	15
SOO	Siret, Orient, Occident, en Espagne	7
SP	Sarre, Art Perse antique	10
SS	Schuckhardt, Schliemann	26
SSC	Siren, Sculpture chinoise	1
SSS	Stuart, Sculp. Stones, Scotland	11
ST	Stradonetz, Antike Terracotten	3
TA	Tacilesco, Adamklissi	2
TAP	Trans. Dep. Archeol., Pennsylvania	8
TDA	Evans, Tomb of Double Axes	4
TM	Tristram, Moab	1
TMMA	Tsountas & Manatt, Myken. Age	2
TS	Toesca, Storia Arte Italiana	2
UC	University College, London	18
WAH	Weber, Arte Ittiti	2
WAI	Westheim, Arte Indica	2
WCR	Wilpert, Catacombe Romane	4
WEM	Woege, Etruskische Malerei	5
WHP	Walters, Hist. Ancient Pottery	1
WM	Wilpert, Römische Mosaiken	7
WPS	Wilson, Preh. Annals, Scotland	4
WS	Wilson, Swastika, U.S. Mus. Rep. 96	1
WSA	Wasmuth, Scultura in Avorio	1
WT	Wace & Thompson, Preh. Thessaly	20
XM	Xanthoudides, Messara	35
ZE	Zeitschrift für Ethnologie	4
⊄	Photographs	138
Sites only quoted		47

CLASSES AND FAMILIES OF ARRANGEMENT.

			No.	Plate.
A		**Hero and Lions, Ishtar.**		
	B	Elamite, Egyptian	2	I
	D	Gilgamesh	3	
	F	Persia to Italy	7	
	H	Hero and bulls, horses, ostriches	5	II
	J	Italian	4	
	K	Heads	2	
	N	Ishtar	4	
	P	Earth goddess, Cybele	3	
	R	Astarte and lions	12	III
	S	Astarte and animals	3	
	U	Goddess and wolves	2	
	V	Goddess and swans	9	
B		**Sphinxes and Animals.**		
	A	Sphinxes and pillar	4	IV
	C	Animals and pillar or plant	5	
	F	Animals and tree	7	
	G	Pair of sphinxes	4	
	J	Pair of lions	3	
	K	Pair of monsters	3	V
	M	Dugong	3	
	N	Sloth head	4	
	O	Stags, cats	2	
	P	Serpents entwined, insects	10	
	Q	Pair of swans	4	
	T	Vase and animals	5	VI
	V	Vase and plant	5	
	W	Vase and birds	9	
C		**Triskele, dragons, nautilus.**		
	B,C	Triskele	17	VII
	D	Three legs	6	
	F	Dragon heads	4	
	H	Chinese dragon	4	
	J	Pair of dolphins	2	
	N	Nautilus	9	
	O	Nautilus shell	3	
	P	Loligo, etc.	8	
	R	Octopus, 8 arms	8	VIII
	S	,, 6 arms	1	
	T	,, 4 arms	4	
	U	,, 2 arms	7	
	X	,, ?	5	
D		**Natural plants.**		
	A	Crocus	4	IX
	C	Pink	3	
	E		5	
	F	Vetch	1	

			No.	Plate.
	G	Star anemone	1	
	H		7	
	J	Lily of the valley	1	
	K		1	
	L	Olive	4	
	M		19	
	N	**Natural plants. Lotus.**		
	N	Palm	1	X
	O	Various	6	
	P	Lotus, natural	1	
	Q	,, grouped	4	
	R	,, Assyrian	5	
	S	,, Italian	5	
	T	,, Greek	1	
	U	,, ,, formal	1	
	W	,, Roman	1	
	X	,, artificial	1	
	Y	,, borders	3	
	Z	,, petals	2	
E		**Lily.**		
	A	Natural	2	XI
	C	Formal	5	
	D	Egyptian	6	
	G	,, formal	8	
	H	Oriental	7	
	J	Flower group	1	
	K	Arborescent	6	
	M	Bowl form, Assyrian	3	
	N	Palmetto, Assyrian	1	XII
	P	,, Cretan, etc.	5	
	Q	,, Italian	6	
	S	Bowl, Italian	8	
	T	Fan, Italian	14	
	Y	Persian, Indian, Byzantine	9	
F		**Palmetto and Formal.**		
	A	Egypt, Assyria	8	XIII
	B	Compound, as capital	7	
	C	Repeated border	18	
	D	Acanthus	9	XIV
	E	,, border	5	
	F	,, debased	7	
	G	Fleur-de-lis	6	XV
	H	Formal flowers	9	
	J	,, borders	10	
	K	Radiate flower	12	XVI
	L	Stem flower	9	
	M	Geometric flower	15	
	N	Vine border	6	

APPROXIMATE RELATIONS OF PERIODS.

EGYPT Dynasty.	B.C.	CRETE.	Bronze. Iron.		BRITAIN	IRELAND	CHINA
	3784						
IV		EM II					
VI							
	3084						
VII		EM III					
XI		MM I					
	2588					2500 Br. I	
XII		MM II	E-B				2203 Hia
	2375						
XIII,XV		MM III	M-B				
XIV,XVI						1900	
XVII		LM I				Br. II	1764 Sheng
	1589						
XVIII		LM II					
A'mhtp. III	1400			Montel. III Br.		1400	
	1328					Br. III	
XIX		LM III	L-B	M. IV Br.			
	1202						
XX				M. V Br.	Beaker A		1120 Chow
	1102						
XXI			E-I			1000 Br. IV	
	950			Hallstatt			
XXII			M-I	I	B	800 Br. V	
XXV							
	664			II			
XXVI			L-I	500 Tène	C	388 Celts	
XXX				250			
	320			II			206 Han
Ptolemaic		Hellenistic		100			
				III			

For the dating in years, see the recent results in *Ancient Egypt*, 1929, June.

AB4

-5000?   GEBEL EL ARAQ   M.P.

ELAMITE WORK IN EGYPT
AT THE CONQUEST S.D.63

B7

S.D.63   HIERAKONPOLIS, QGH, LXXVI
-5000?
EGYPTIAN COPY

D3

H.W.159

GILGAMESH

F2

PERSIAN CYL. HW,1108

D6

HW.165

D8

OVERHEAD
M.I.A.II, i

CRETE, IDEAN CAVE

ASSYRIAN INFLUENCE IN CRETE
GILGAMESH AND THE BULL

F3

CORINTH AZ·1884·VIII

F4

-400? DORYLAION
MAIA 1895 I

F6

NINEVEH L·NII·64

F7

-500   SEALING MEMPHIS   P.W.M,XXXVI

F8

BRONZE, SABAEAN   N·A·A·67

F9

BRONZE, PERUGIA,   M.I.252.17

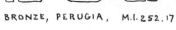

H1

-350 ATHENS, MARBLE THRONE, MAIA,1926,124

H3

-730 NIMRUD   L·N·XLViii

A H5
-730   NIMRUD EMBROIDERY   LN·XLIV

H7
-700   OWNER URZANA   M·O·D·282 C   H.W·42

H9
SUBDUING HORSES, H·W·1109

J2
BRONZE, SABAEAN, N·A·A·68

J4
BOLOGNA   M·I·100.

J6
-300? ARCEVIA   M·I·152

J8
GOLD RELIEF   M·I·367
PRAENESTE, BERNARDINI, P.O·133

K4
+265 To 300   SAC·XL
CHINA

K7
~250   SCV,130

EARTH GODDESS AND LIONS

P3
AMARI CRETE
JHS·1925·66

ISHTAR AND LIONS

N2
HW·412

N4
HW 407

N6
HW 135a

N8
HW 129a

P6
BOEOTIA   MATA·1925·161

P8
PHRYGIA   HOC 39

ISHTAR-ASTARTE AND LIONS

R5
-550 KUBAN   R·I·G·VI

R10
SPARTA   J·H·S·

R15
MOD·281a

R20
RHODES, B.M

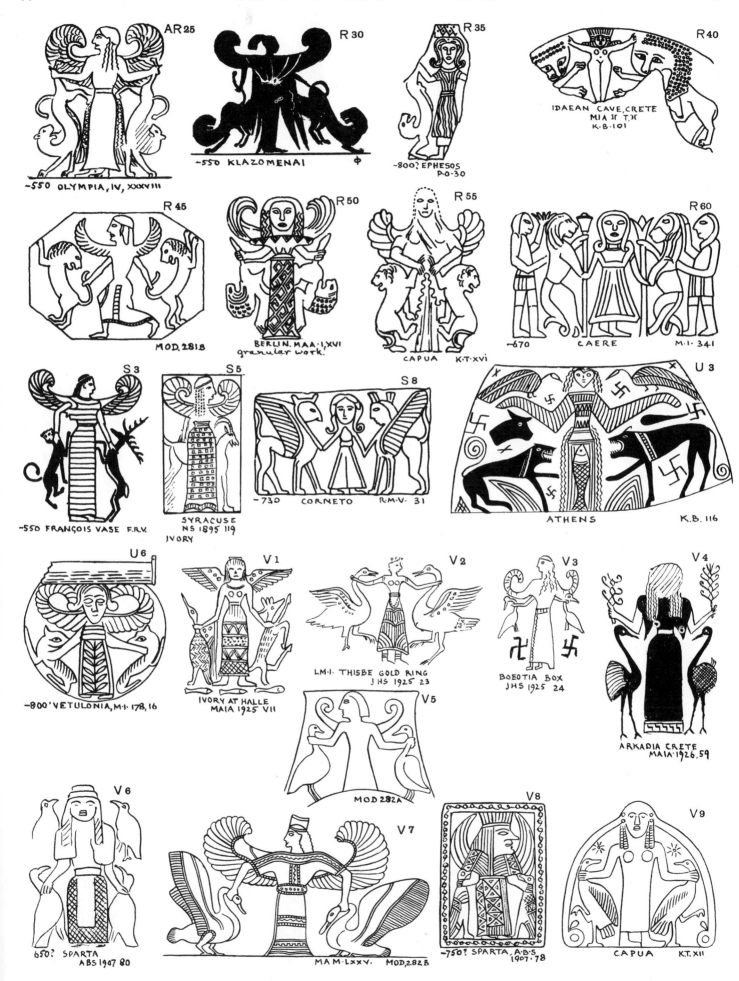

AR 25
-550 OLYMPIA, IV, XXXVIII

R 30
-550 KLAZOMENAI

R 35
-800? EPHESOS
P.O.30

R 40
IDAEAN CAVE, CRETE
MIA II T.X
K·B·101

R 45
MOD.281B

R 50
BERLIN. MAA·I,XVI
granular work.

R 55
CAPUA   K.T.XVI

R 60
-670   CAERE   M·I·341

S 3
-550 FRANÇOIS VASE F.R.V.

S 5
SYRACUSE
NS 1895 119
IVORY

S 8
-730   CORNETO   R·M·V· 31

U 3
ATHENS   K.B. 116

U 6
-800 VETULONIA, M·I· 178, 16

V 1
IVORY AT HALLE
MAIA 1925 VII

V 2
LM·I· THISBE GOLD RING
JHS 1925 23

V 3
BOEOTIA BOX
JHS 1925 24

V 4
ARKADIA CRETE
MAIA·1926,59

V 5
MOD 282A

V 6
650? SPARTA
ABS 1907 80

V 7
MAM·LXXV·   MOD.282B

V 8
-750? SPARTA, A.B.S
1907· 78

V 9
CAPUA   K.T. XII

BA2

MYKENAE, RING F.G.

A6

−600? MEGARA HYBLA·MA 1899.762

A4

−550   R·I·G·Vi
KUBAN
SIBERIAN BEAST BELOW

A8

+1000? ATHENS, VERGINE GORGOPICO
DESCENT FROM BC6.   R·A·L· 281

C6

MYKENAE   T·M·M·A·

C9

BOLOGNA B·G93

C2

MYKENAE   φ

C4

CERVETRI M·1·335·5

C8

XVII   AKKER MON·DIV·51
EARLIEST LILY GROUP, ASIATIC? SEE ED2

F1

PRE,1. EGYPT   C·DA,162,164

F2

−3500   UR   I·L·N·28

F3

−550
KUBAN, AXE·RIG·viii

F4

−200 SENDJERLI WAI·xLii

F5

SALETTA BOLOGNA
RV II Li

F7

−730   NIMRUD, DRESS   L·N·L

F9

−1800 BERLIN BOWL   M·S·11

G2

−550   R·I·G· Vi
KUBAN
ASIATIC GRYPHON BELOW

G4

−550 NOICATTARO, GBA XVII

G6

CAPUA   K·T·XII·3
BOLD U DOLFIN SITULA   B·C·
CAULONIA MA 1914 765
ROME CONSERVATORI·S·T· Lxii

G8

−350   ESTE   M·A· X

J3

−550, NOICATTARO   GBA
XVII

J5

SUSA CYLINDER, H·W/1217

J7

SUSA CYLINDER   H·W·1218

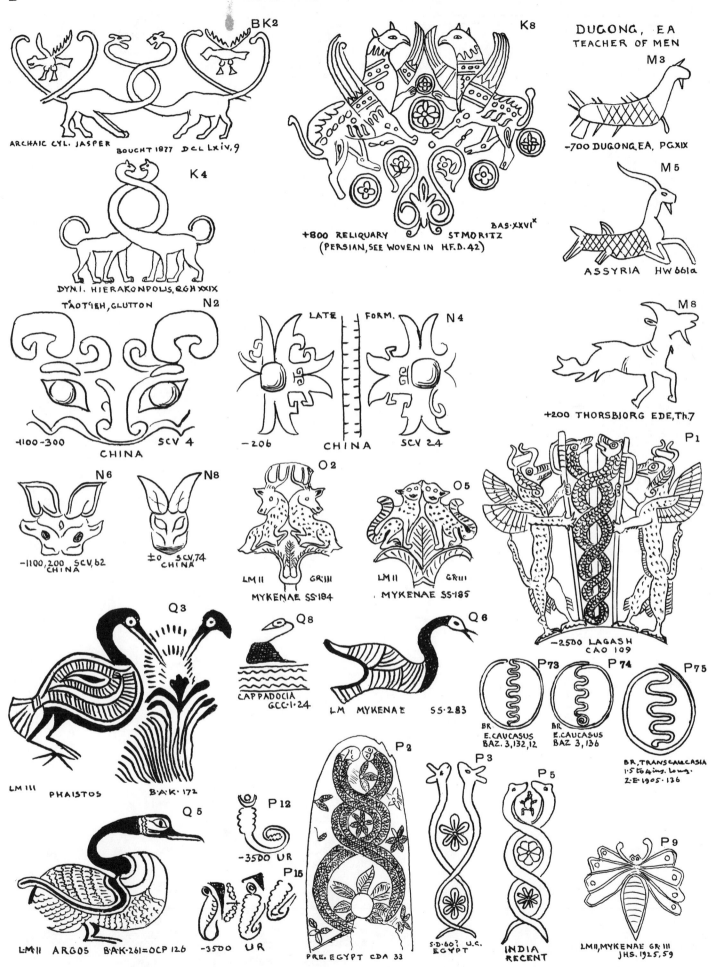

BK2
ARCHAIC CYL. JASPER   BOUCHT 1877 DCL LXIV, 9

K4
DYN. I. HIERAKONPOLIS, QGH XXIX

K8

DUGONG, EA
TEACHER OF MEN
M3
-700 DUGONG, EA, PGXIX

M5
ASSYRIA   HW 661a

+800 RELIQUARY   ST MORITZ   BAS. XXVIᵡ
(PERSIAN, SEE WOVEN IN H.F.D. 42)

T'AOT'IEH, GLUTTON   N2
-1100-300   SCV 4
CHINA

LATE   FORM.   N4
-206   CHINA   SCV 24

M8
+200 THORSBJORG EDE, Th. 7

N6
-1100, 200   SCV, 62
CHINA

N8
±0.   SCV, 74
CHINA

O2
LM II   GR III
MYKENAE SS·184

O5
LM II   GRⅡ
MYKENAE SS-185

P1
-2500 LAGASH
CAO 109

Q3
LM III   PHAISTOS   B·A·K· 172

Q8
CAPPADOCIA
GCC·1·24

Q6
LM MYKENAE   SS·283

P73
BR
E.CAUCASUS
BAZ 3,132,12

P74
BR
E.CAUCASUS
BAZ 3,136

P75
BR, TRANSCAUCASIA
1·5 to 4 ins. long.
Z·E·1905·136

Q5
LM·II ARGOS   B·A·K·261=OCP 126

P12
-3500 UR

P15
-3500   UR

P2
PRE. EGYPT CDA 33

P3
S·D·60? U·C.
EGYPT

P5
INDIA
RECENT

P9
LM II, MYKENAE GR III
JHS. 1925, 59

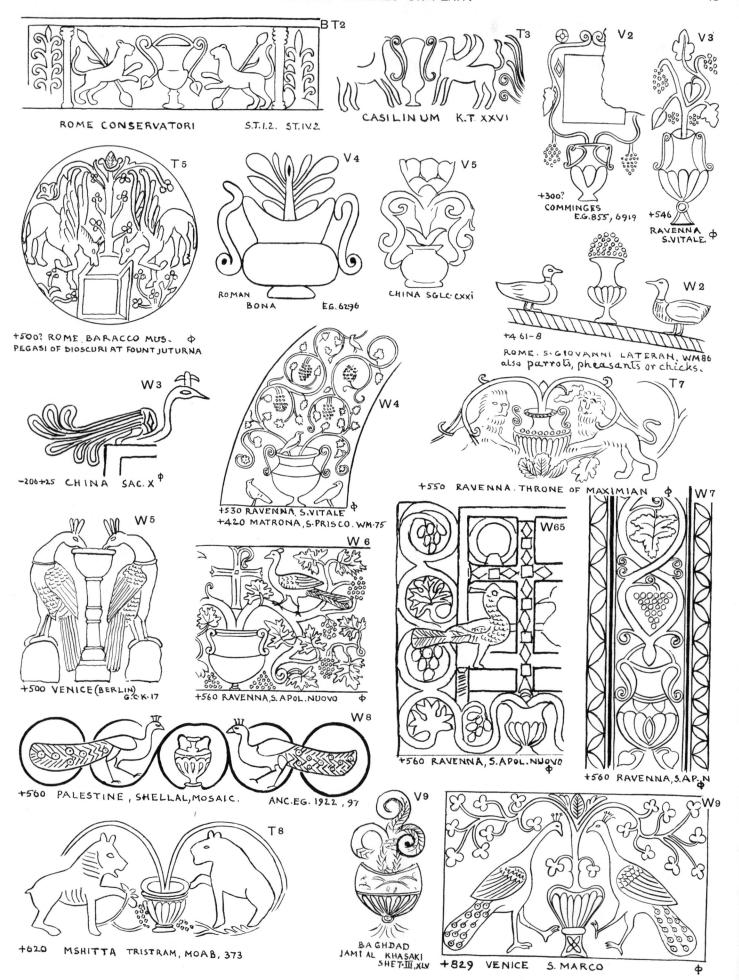

BT2
ROME CONSERVATORI   S.T.I.2.   ST.IV.2.

T3
CASILINUM   K.T. XXVI

V2
V3
+300? COMMINGES   E.G.855, 6919
+546 RAVENNA S.VITALE.

T5
+500? ROME. BARACCO MUS.
PEGASI OF DIOSCURI AT FOUNT JUTURNA

V4
ROMAN BONA   E.G. 6296

V5
CHINA SGLC.CXXI

W2
+461-8
ROME. S.GIOVANNI LATERAN. WM86
also parrots, pheasants or chicks.

W3
-206+25 CHINA SAC.X

W4
+530 RAVENNA, S.VITALE
+420 MATRONA, S.PRISCO. WM.75

T7
+550 RAVENNA. THRONE OF MAXIMIAN

W5
+500 VENICE (BERLIN) G.C.K.17

W6
+560 RAVENNA, S.APOL.NUOVO

W65
+560 RAVENNA, S.APOL.NUOVO

W7
+560 RAVENNA, S.AP.N

W8
+560 PALESTINE, SHELLAL, MOSAIC.   ANC.EG. 1922, 97

T8
+620 MSHITTA TRISTRAM, MOAB, 373

V9
BAGHDAD JAMI AL KHASAKI SHET.III.XLV

W9
+829 VENICE S. MARCO

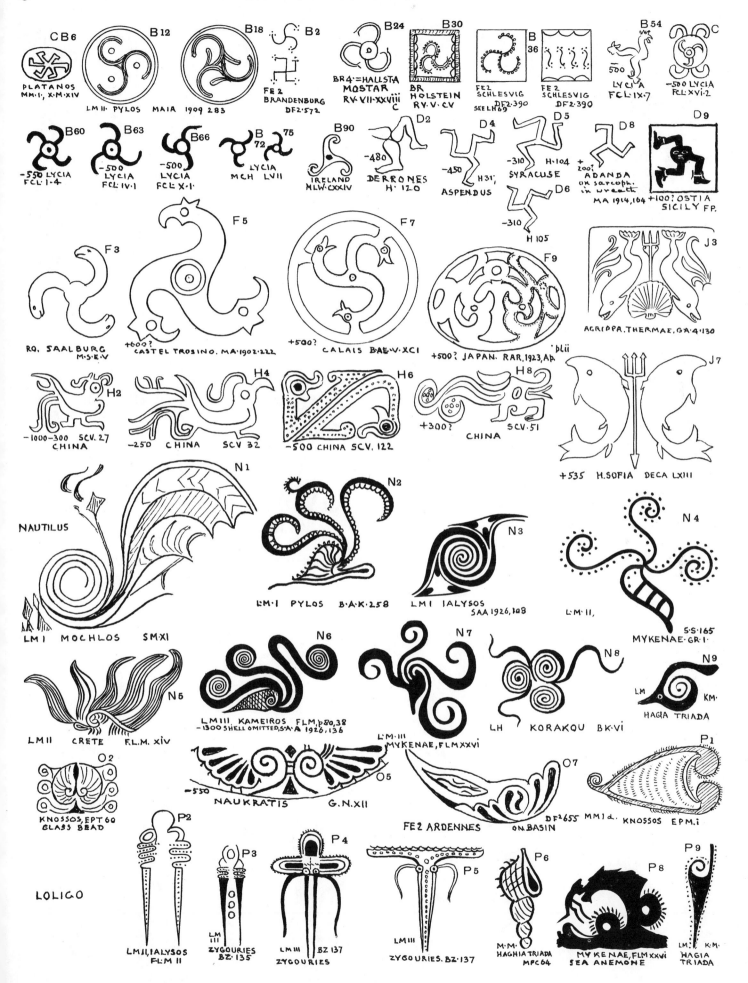

CB6 PLATANOS MM·I·, X·M·XIV

B12 LM II· PYLOS

B18 MAIA 1909 283

B2 FE 2 BRANDENBURG DF2·572

B24 BR4·=HALLSTA MOSTAR RV·VII·XXVIII C

B30 BR HOLSTEIN RV·V·CV

B 36 FE2 SCHLESVIG SEE LH69

FE2 SCHLESVIG DF2·390

B54 −500 LYCIA FCL·IX·7

C −500 LYCIA FCL·XVI·2

B60 −550 LYCIA FCL·I·4

B63 −500 LYCIA FCL·IV·1

B66 −500 LYCIA FCL·X·1·

B 72 LYCIA MCH·LVII

75

B90 IRELAND MLW·CXXIV

D2 −480 DERRONES H·120

D4 −450 ASPENDUS H·31

D5 −310 SYRACUSE H·104

D6 −310 H·105

D8 +200? ADANDA ON sarcoph. in wreath MA 1914,164

D9 +100? OSTIA SICILY F.P.

F3 RO. SAALBURG M·S·E·V

F5 +600? CASTEL TROSINO. MA·1902·222

F7 +500? CALAIS BAE·V·XCI

F9 +500? JAPAN. RAR,1923,AA ·plii

J3 AGRIPPA. THERMAE. GA·4·130

H2 −1000−300 SCV. 27 CHINA

H4 −250 CHINA SCV 32

H6 −500 CHINA SCV. 122

H8 +300? CHINA SCV·51

J7 +535 H.SOFIA DECA LXIII

NAUTILUS

N1 LM I MOCHLOS SM·XI

N2 LM·I PYLOS B·A·K·258

N3 LMI IALYSOS SAA 1926,108

N4 L·M·II, MYKENAE·GR·I·

S·S·165

N5 LM II CRETE F.L.M. XIV

N6 LM III KAMEIROS FLM,p80,38 −1300 SHELL OMITTED,S·A·A 1926,136

N7 L·M·III MYKENAE,FLMXXVI

N8 LH KORAKOU BK·VI

N9 LM KM· HAGIA TRIADA

O2 KNOSSOS, EPT 60 GLASS BEAD

O5 −550 NAUKRATIS G.N.XII

O7 FE2 ARDENNES ON BASIN DF2655

P1 MMId. KNOSSOS EPM.i

LOLIGO

P2 LMII,IALYSOS FLM II

P3 LM III ZYGOURIES BZ·135

P4 LM III ZYGOURIES BZ 137

P5 LMIII ZYGOURIES. BZ·137

P6 M·M· HAGHIA TRIADA MPC64

P8 MYKENAE,FLMXXVI SEA ANEMONE

P9 LM· K·M· HAGIA TRIADA

CR2

L.M.IB GOURNIA, B.H.G.

R3

LMII

MYKENAE GRIII SS190

R4

MM·KAMARES ODE XI

R5

MYKENAE, GRIII
SS·188

R6

KUPHONISIA MGP 307
AMORGOS

R8

DIPYLON MAIA. 1907 XXV

R26

MYKENAE
STONE BOX EPH·1888

R9

+265 TO 589 S·A·C XXVI
"MADE BY FAN FAMILY OF SUNG" IN HONAN

T2

LM II IALYSOS FLM XIV
LM III GOURNIA. BHGX. SEE SAA 1926 79

S2

·M III MPC. 127

U1

~1350 MYKENAE
ABS 1923 107

T4

LM II IALYSOS F.L.M·Viii

T5

LM II IALYSOS FLM·ii

U2

LM II IALYSOS, FLM ii

U3

LM·HAGIA TRIADA. K·M·

T6

LOS
MILLARES
SPAIN S·O·O·iii

U6

LH III KORAKOU BK91

U9

MEGALITH
PERIOD C·D·133
CUP
BRETON

U7

LH III
=1150 PALEST. BK·85
KORAKOU

U8

S·A·A·1926,43

X2

CRETE
M·S·X

X3

HITTITE
H.H. 135

X5

ORSOVA
M·B·H·1912,15,16

X6

X8

KNOSSOS
INLAY
E.P.T·40

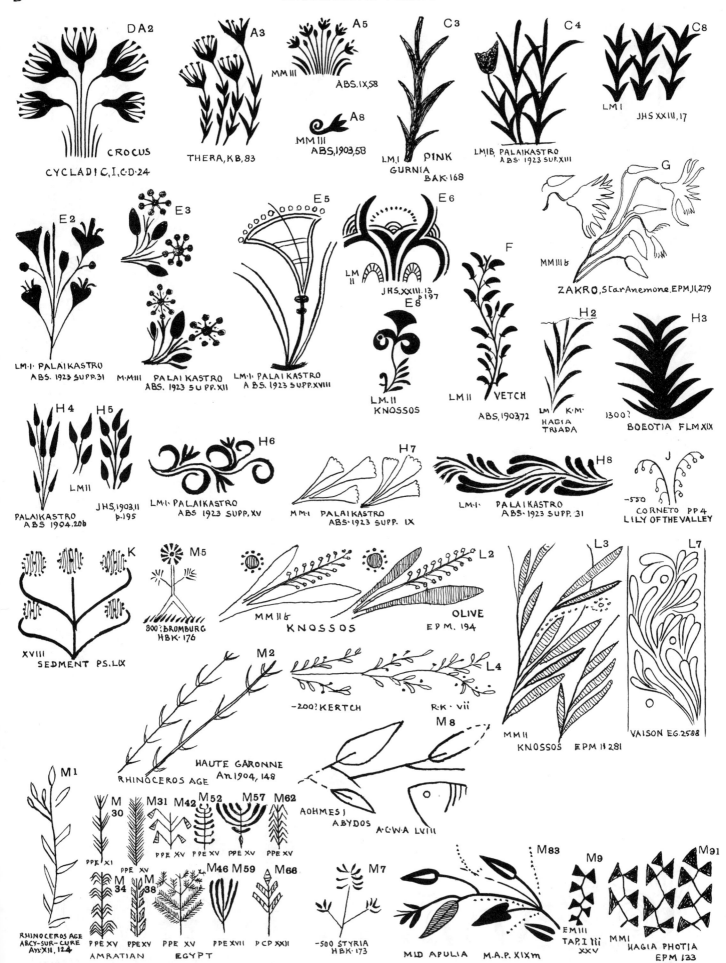

DA2
CROCUS
CYCLADIC, I, C.D.24

A3
THERA, KB, 83

A5
MM III
ABS.IX,58

A8
MM III
ABS,1903,58

C3
LM.I PINK
GURNIA
BAK·168

C4
LM·IB, PALAIKASTRO
ABS·1923 SUP.XIII

C8
LM I
JHS XXIII, 17

E2
LM·I· PALAIKASTRO
ABS. 1923 SUPR.31

E3
M·M III PALAIKASTRO
ABS. 1923 SUPP.XII

E5
LM·I· PALAIKASTRO
A BS. 1923 SUPP.XVIII

E6
LM II
JHS.XXIII.13
p.197

E8
LM.II
KNOSSOS

F
LM II VETCH
ABS, 1903 72

G
MM III b
ZAKRO, Star Anemone. EPM.II,279

H2
LM K·M·
HAGIA TRIADA

H3
1300?
BOEOTIA FLM XIX

H4 H5
PALAIKASTRO
ABS 1904.20b
LM II
JHS,1903,11
p·195

H6
LM·I· PALAIKASTRO
ABS 1923 SUPP.XV

H7
MM·I PALAIKASTRO
ABS·1923 SUPP. IX

H8
LM·I· PALAIKASTRO
ABS·1923 SUPP. 31

J
-550
CORNETO PP4
LILY OF THE VALLEY

K
XVIII
SEDMENT PS.LIX

M5
800?BROMBURG
HBK·176

L2
MM II b KNOSSOS
OLIVE
EPM. 194

L3

L7
VAISON EG.2588

M2
-200? KERTCH
HAUTE GARONNE
An.1904, 148
RHINOCEROS AGE

L4
R·K· vii

M8
MM II KNOSSOS EPM II 281

M1
RHINOCEROS AGE
ARCY-SUR-CURE
An.XII.124

M 30
PPE XI

M31 M42 M52 M57 M62
PPE XV PPE XV PPE XV PPE XV

M 34 M 38
PPE XV PPE XV
AMRATIAN

M46 M59 M66
PPE XV PPE XVII P CP XXII
EGYPT

M7
-500 STYRIA
HBK·173

AOHMES I
ABYDOS
A·G·W·A LVIII

M83
MLD APULIA
M.A.P. XIXm

M9
EM III
TAP.I III
xxv

M91
MM I HAGIA PHOTIA
EPM I33

M7 CYPRUS. LOUVRE K.B.108 D.C.P.232

KOUYUNJIK N

P1 UNIT OF NECKLACE KYRENIA, CYPRUS S.A. VIII

P3 CRETE. M.S. XI

P5 TAMASSOS. MAK323

P7 CRETE M.S. XI

P A P9 CYPRUS   M.A.K. 322

Q2 SUPERPOSED IN PILE. RUAD +WINGED SPHINK ASSYRIAN STYLE R.M.P. IV

Q4 -700? MARINO LAZIALE TOMB 16 BRONZE 1923 K.M.

Q5 FALERII M.1.311 11. K.M.

Q6 -600? CAPENA (ROMA) K.M.

Q8 -600? MUS. GREG.

Q9 F.P. - -700? ATHENS. K.B.116

S2 +100? MATHURA. BOSTON. Φ

S3 VULCI M.1.264.8

S4 S5 -670 BARBERINI TOMB, PRAENESTE IMPRESSED GOLD M.A.A. V 8

S6 MARZABOTTO. M.1.107,15

S7 -600? CAPENA (ROMA) K.M.

S8 -600? CAPENA K.M.

S9 DAN II RÖSSEN -2000 CDP 118

T2 TARQINII MKE 89 B.MUS.

T3 CORNETO M.1.294

T4 +400 NICHOMACHORUM DIPTYCH D.C.D. LIV

T5 CAPUA. K.T.109

T6 -300? MARNE   H.J. II.184

T66 -650? M.1.243

T7 CAPUA K.T.XXV

T74 -600? CRETE K.B.115

T8 M.1 1914 VETULONIA, LICTOR.

T85 GHIUSI, PANIA M.1.225.7

T9 +90 CRYPTOPORTICUS PALATINE M.A.A. IV, XI

T93- +50 SEBASTIANO CATACOMB, ROME.

T95 F.P. +130 COL.TRAIAN, G.A.117

Y3 +546 S. VITALE RAVENNA Φ

Y1

T97 +150 PANCRATII TOMB M.A.A. IV.XXXIII

+620, ANAHITA TAQ I BUSTAN DRESS H.F.D. LXV

Y2 + 546 S. VITALE, RAVEN. R.S.79

Y4 +450 AJANTA, C.I.P.31 INDIA

Y5 +525 DIPTYCH PHILOXENUS D.C.D XXX

Y9 DENMARK. M.A.K.224

Y6 +706 S. MARIA, ANTICA. ROME Φ

Y7 +750 S. MARIA, ANTICA ROME F.P.

Y8 +770 S. MARIA CIVIDALE Φ

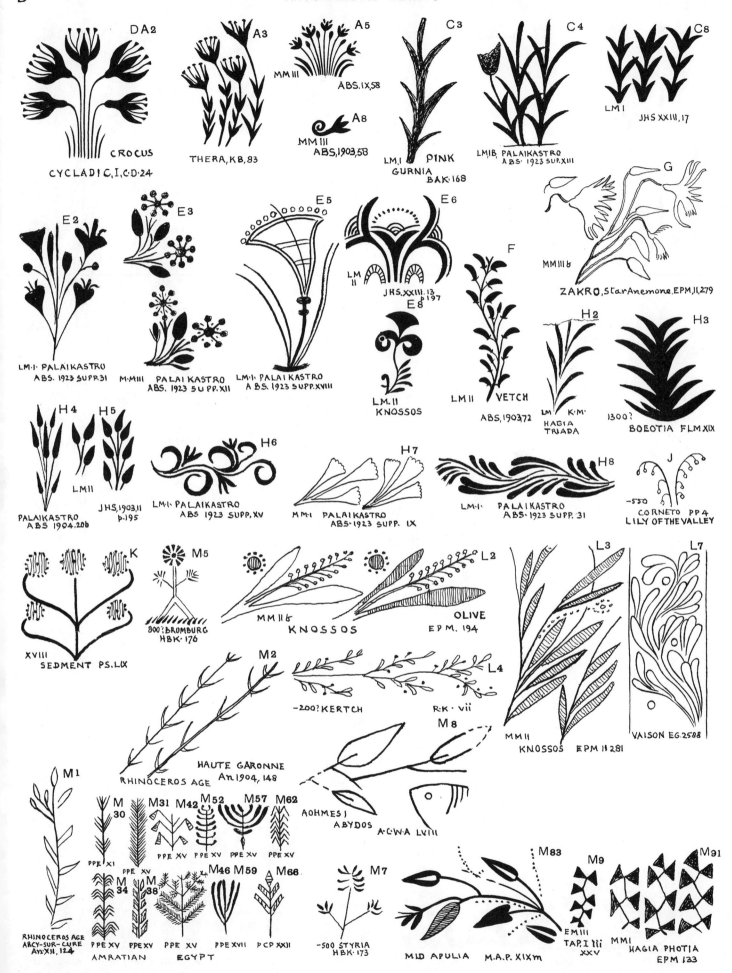

DA2
CROCUS
CYCLADIC, I.C.D.24

A3
THERA, KB, 83

A5
MM III
ABS.IX,58

A8
MM III
ABS,1903,58

C3
LM I PINK
GURNIA BAK·168

C4
LMIB, PALAIKASTRO
ABS·1923 SUP.XIII

C8
LM I
JHS XXIII, 17

E2
LM·I· PALAIKASTRO
ABS. 1923 SUPR.31

E3
M·M III PALAIKASTRO
ABS. 1923 SUPP.XII

E5
LM·I· PALAIKASTRO
A BS. 1923 SUPP.XVIII

E6
LM II
JHS.XXIII.13
p.197

E8
LM. II
KNOSSOS

F
LM II VETCH
ABS, 1903,72

G
MM III b
ZAKRO, StarAnemone.EPM,II,279

H2
LM K·M·
HAGIA TRIADA

H3
1300?
BOEOTIA FI.M XIX

H4 H5
LM II
PALAIKASTRO
ABS 1904,20b
JHS,1903,11
p·195

H6
LM·I· PALAIKASTRO
ABS 1923 SUPP. XV

H7
MM·I· PALAIKASTRO
ABS·1923 SUPP. IX

H8
LM·I· PALAIKASTRO
ABS· 1923 SUPP. 31

J
−550
CORNETO PP 4
LILY OF THE VALLEY

K
XVIII
SEDMENT PS.LIX

M5
800?BROMBURG
HBK·176

L2
MM II b KNOSSOS
OLIVE
EPM. 194

L3

L7

M2
HAUTE GARONNE
An 1904, 148
RHINOCEROS AGE

L4
−200?KERTCH
R·K· vii

M8
AOHMES I
ABYDOS
A·C·W·A LVIII

MM II KNOSSOS EPM II 281

VAISON EG.2588

M1
RHINOCEROS AGE
ARCY-SUR-CURE
An·XII,124

M 30
PPE XI

M31 M42 M52 M57 M62
PPE XV PPE XV PPE XV PPE XV

M 34 M 38
PPE XV PPE XV
AMRATIAN

M46 M59 M66
PPE XV PPE XVII P CP XXII
EGYPT

M7
−500 STYRIA
HBK·173

M83
MID APULIA
M.A.P. XIX m

M9
EM III
TAP.I III
XXV

M91
MM I
HAGIA PHOTIA
EPM 123

DN

O2

O3

O4

O5

+600?

SASSANIDE BOWL. SP. CXXIII

O7

O9

+488 DIPTYCH SIVIDIUS DCD VIII

L·M·   K·M·
HAGIA TRIADA

+50? MAINZ   L.A.V. 502

NEUMAGEN E.G 5220

L·M II

PYLOS MAIA 1909 XXII

-100 COMMAGENE ON DRESS SP. LVII

LOTUS

P

1450 (BERLIN)   M.S.9

Q2

XVIII AMARNA P.A.XIX

Q4

XVIII GUROB P.I·K· XX

Q7

-1180 GERAR   P.G.I

R1

ARCHAIC.SUSA.DCL.XV,8

Q9

+589 TO 616 CHINA SAC XLVII

R4

KOUYUNJIK

R6

730 NIMRUD EMBROIDERY, LN.XLIV

R7

ASHUR ACA.XIV

R9

LITOY KURGAN LOW DNIEPER SKYTHO-SARM· RV·XIII,XXXIV A

S2

-600 CORTONA   MA 1925,110

CAPUA   KT·41

S4

CAPUA   KT.42

S5

S6

TORCELLO   Φ

T

-700 RHODES   KB.115

S8

CAPUA   K T.XXXIV

U

-600 SPARTA, ABS 1909.31

Y5

-550 NAUKRATIS PNKVIII

Z2

XVIII AMARNA   P.A. X

X

-600 NAUKRATIS   PNK.VI,& XIII

W

+500 RAVENNA THEODORIC. MA 1916 755

Y4

-600 CORNETO, PP.2

Y7

-550 NAUKRATIS PNK. VIII S·APULIA

Z8

450 BOLOGNA   R·I.35
   MA XXVIII

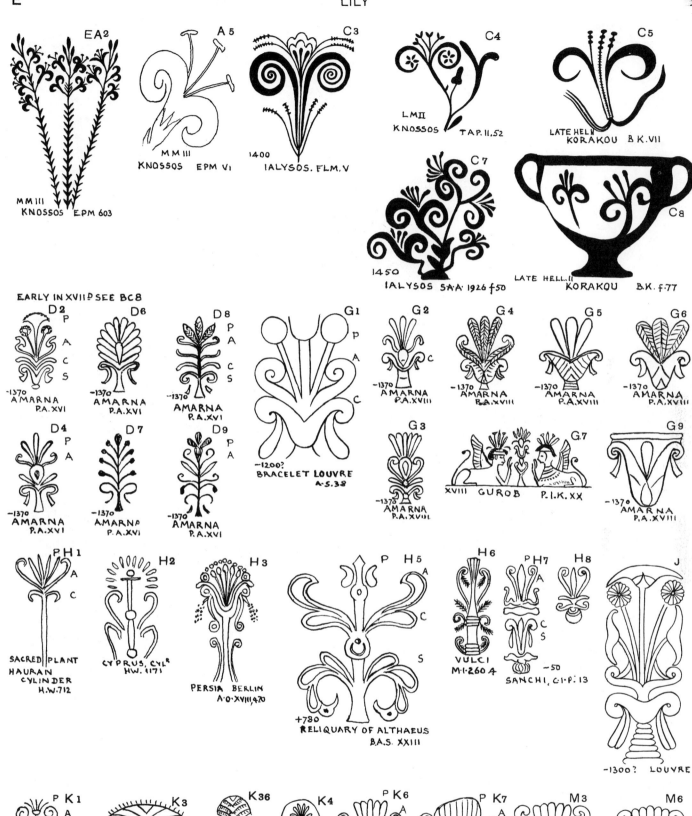

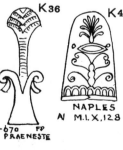

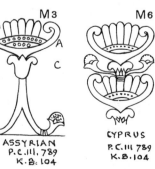

M7 CYPRUS, LOUVRE K.B.108 D.C.P.232

N KOUYUNJIK

P1 UNIT OF NECKLACE KYRENIA, CYPRUS S.A.VIII ?+200

P3 CRETE.MS.51

P5 TAMASSOS.MAK323

P7 CRETE MS.XI

P P9 A

CYPRUS M.A.K.322

Q2 SUPERPOSED IN PILE. RUAD +WINGED SPHINX ASSYRIAN STYLE R.M.P. IV

Q4 -700? MARINO LAZIALE TOMB 16 BRONZE 1923 K.M.

Q5 FALERII M.I.311 II. K.M.

Q6 -600? CAPENA (ROMA) K.M.

Q8 -600? MUS.GREG.

Q9 F.P.- -700? ATHENS.K.B.116

S2 +100? MATHURA, BOSTON. Φ

S3 VULCI M.I.264.8

S4 -670 S5 BARBERINI TOMB, PRAENESTE IMPRESSED GOLD M.A.A.V 8

S6 MARZABOTTO, M.I.107,15

S7 -600? CAPENA(ROMA) K.M.

S8 -600? CAPENA K.M.

S9 DAN B RÖSSEN -2000 CDP 118

T2 TARQINII MKE 89 B·MUS·

T3 CORNETO M.I.294

T4 +400 NICHOMACHORUM DIPTYCH D.C.D. LIV

T5 CAPUA. K.T.109

T6 -300? MARNE H.J. II.184

T66 -650? M.I.243

T7 CAPUA K.T.XXV

T74 -600? CRETE K.B.115

T8 M.I 1914 VETULONIA, LICTOR.

T 85 GHIUSI, PANIA M.I.225.7

Y3

T9 +90 CRYPTOPORTICUS PALATINE M.A.A, IV, XI

+50 SEBASTIANO CATACOMB, ROME.

T93 F.P.+130

T95 COL.TRAIAN, G.A.117

Y1 +620, ANAHITA TAQ I BUSTAN DRESS H.F.D.LXV

Y3 +546 S.VITALE Φ RAVENNA

Y4 +450 AJANTA, C.I.P.31 INDIA

Y5 +525 DIPTYCH PHILOXENUS D.C.D XXX

Y9 DENMARK. M.A.K.224

T97 +150 PANCRATII TOMB M.A.A.IV.XXXIII

Y2 + 546, S.VITALE, RAVEN R.S.79

Y6 +706 S.MARIA, ANTICA. ROME Φ

Y7 S.MARIA, ANTICA ROME F.P.

Y8 +770 S.MARIA CIVIDALE Φ

FA1

X DYN QAU   PQ i

A3

−730 NIMRUD EMBROIDERY   L.N. VI

A4

NIMRUD   BRIT. MUS. P.O.9

A9

LITOY KURGAN LOW DNIEPR
SCYTHO-SARM. RVXIII 34A

A5

ASSYRIA BM

A6

SIBERIA
MPO III 224

A7

THRONE ROOM BABYLON
KWE 64

A8

−500? SUSA LION FRIEZE S.P. XXXIX

B1

−570 AOHMES
MON. LEYDEN
II, LXVII

B2

KOLDEWY BABYLON, 130
KWE 64

B3

−700,600   MEGIDDO

B4

CHIUSI. (FLOR.) DA.83

B5

−600? CORNETO   Φ

B8

MONTE CALVARIO
NS.1905, 233

B9

−670 CAERE
R·M·E

C2

M.I. 244

C7

−700 CUMA. MA,1913 XLVIII

C12

NIMRUD, MAK, 963

C22

FALERII   M.I. 327.13

C32

−670 CAERE RME

C37

C17

−600?
CERVETRI SEDIA CORSINI
MA 1916, 458, V

C27

CHIUSI. PANIA   M·I·225.7.

PRAENESTE, BARBERINI TOMB
ROUGH IVORY.   M·A·A·V. 10

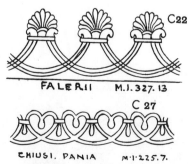

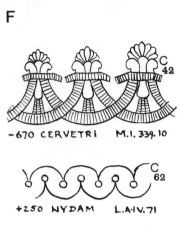

-670 CERVETRI M.I. 339.10

FALERII, M.I. 319.2

FALERII M.I.3II,18

FALERII M.I.3 II.19

+250 NYDAM L.A.IV.71

HANGEBEKENS, SWEDEN
M.L.S. V

CAPUA KT.XXVIII

NAGY SZENT MIKLOS S.A.65
GOLD BOTTLE

+800 AGAUNE, RELIQUARY
(SEE DACIAN QC 4,5) BAS.XXV

MONTE CALVARIO
N.S. 1905, 232 fig. 26

ACANTHUS

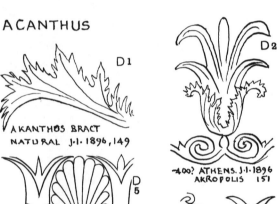

AKANTHOS BRACT
NATURAL J.I. 1896,149

-400? ATHENS. J.I.1896
AKROPOLIS 151

-400 ERECHTHEION. K.B.138

-500 CAULONIA, MA, 1923, IV

-400? CAULONIA. MA.1923,VII

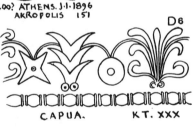

CAPUA. KT. XXX

CAPUA KT.XXV

ST, III, I

SITULA
BOLDU-
-DOLFIN
B.C.66

CORNETO W.E.M. VIII

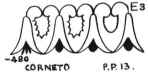

-480 CORNETO P.P. 13.

S.APULIA
M.A.p.XXVIII,3

-250
N.APULIA
R.M.I.46

CAPUA KT. 45

+1050 S.CLEMENTE, ROME. ALEXIS Φ

+160 BAALBEK, ALTAR COURT.

S.B.I.103
+200 COTTAEUM
JRS 1925 XXIII

YUDINA
M.M. XV

+640 SYRACUSE
JAMB Φ

+640 Φ
SYRACUSE
JAMB

FOSCHERARI BOLOGNA Φ

FLEUR-DE-LIS

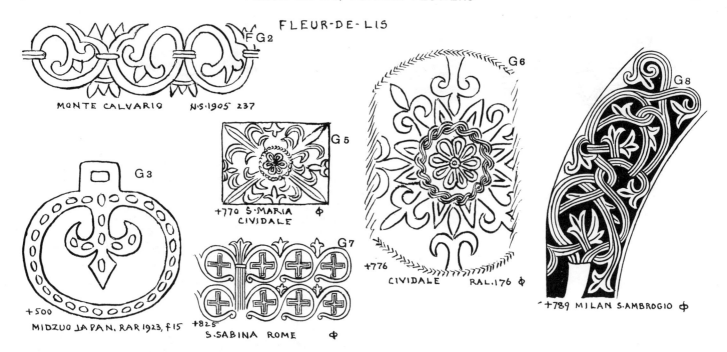

MONTE CALVARIO   N.S.1905 237   FG2

G3

G5   +770 S.MARIA CIVIDALE

G6   +776 CIVIDALE   RAL.176 φ

G8   +789 MILAN S.AMBROGIO φ

+500   MIDZUO JAPAN, RAR 1923, f15

G7   +825 S.SABINA ROME φ

FORMAL FLOWERS

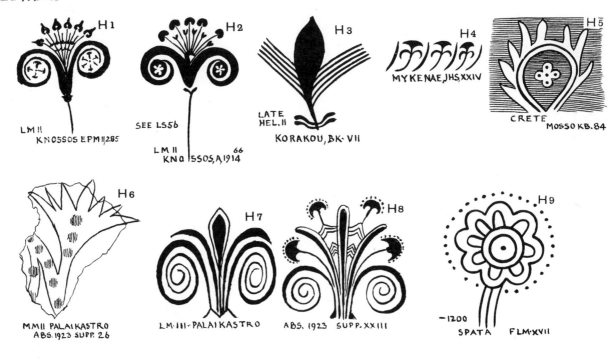

H1   LM II   KNOSSOS EPM II 285

H2   SEE LS5b   LM II   KNOSSOS, A 1914 66

H3   LATE HEL. II   KORAKOU, BK. VII

H4   MYKENAE, JHS XXIV

H̄5   CRETE   MOSSO KB. 84

H6   MM II PALAIKASTRO ABS. 1923 SUPP. 26

H7   LM III PALAIKASTRO

H8   ABS. 1923 SUPP. XXIII

H9   -1200   SPATA   FLM XVII

J3   -670 CUMA   R.M.I. 53

J6   -400 ARCHENA, MURCIA R.V.I x Lii

J4   -670 CUMA   M.A.1913,30; R.M.I. ϸL.36

J5

J7   MM III KNOSSOS FAIENCE ABS 1903 67

J73   XVII KAMES SPEAR ESB 30

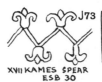

J74   MYKENAE

J8   LM II BSA 1903 ϸ311, g.

J9   LM II PYLOS, MAIA 1909 290

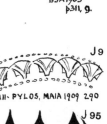

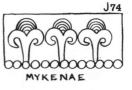

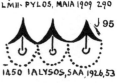

J95   1450 IALYSOS, SAA 1926, 53

FK1 — MM·I· PALAIKASTRO ABS·1923 SUPP·VI·

K2 — MM PHAESTOS MPC, 13

K3 — XVIII AMARNA P.A.XXVII

K35 — LM III2 IALYSOS FLM VIII

K4 — XVIII L·M·II AMARNA P.A.XVIII

K5 — XVIII AMARNA PA.XXVII

K6 — LM I a KNOSSOS EPM II 285 −1400

K63 — IALYSOS, FLM, III

K68 — MYKENAE FLM, XXXV

K7 — −1150? CRETE MA.1889, 230, II

K8 — MYKENAE FLM, XXXIV

K9 — −1400 IALYSOS, FLM, VI

L1 — XII EGYPT UC

L2 — CRETE, EPM15

L3 — XII SCARAB EPM.150

L4 — MM I. CRETE M.S. XII

L5 **L6** — 1400 IALYSOS, FLM III AND IX

L7 — 1350 ALIKI, ATTICA FLM.XVIII

L8 — LM III COZZO, SYRACUSE / MA,1893 I, DCP 153

L9 — CROSS OF JUSTIN + SOPHIA LATERAN·DECA·IXI

M1 — MM I· PLATANOS X·M·XIV

M2 — MM I. PALAI KASTRO ABS·1923 SUPP.VIII

M25 — −1400? CRETE / FLM XIV

M31 — ARCEVIA MA.1900, 694·

M35 **M36** **M38** — LM II KNOSSOS HOUSES TAP. II 60

M50 — POMPEI B P.

M54 — AQUILEIA RS. 83

M58 — +630 CROWN OF SWINTILA. RS. 100

M60 — LM.I. MA.1902.VIII

M65 — +620 TAQI BUSTAN S P.XCII

M70 — FRANK WIESBADEN AFW 160

M75 — +660 FRIESLAND, A.A.S. 295

M90 — +800 SWISS BINDING B.A.S. XXVˣ

N2 — +810 RAVENNA S.APOL.CLASSE Φ

N3 — BAALBEK, ALTAR COURT SB. I· 83

N4 — +300? GRADINA MBH· 1906, 244

N5 — +560 RAVENNA, S.APOLLINARE NUOVO Φ

N7 — +500 RAVENNA ARIAN BAPTISTY Φ

N9 — 850 DEIR ES SURIANI EGYPT GC K. 60

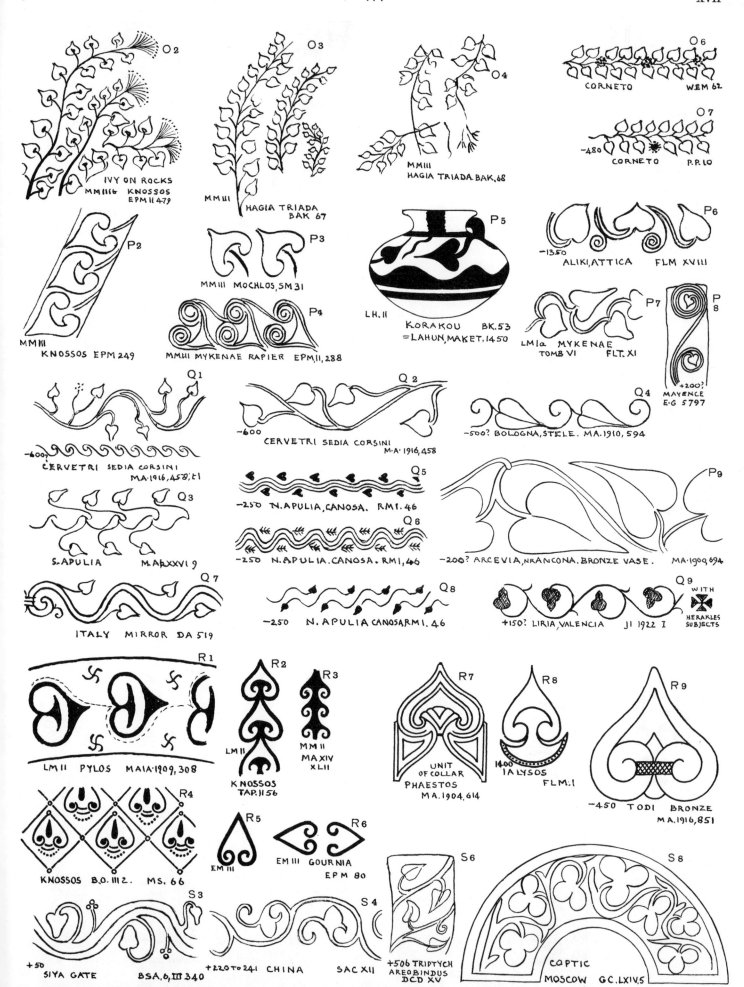

O2

O3

O4

O6
CORNETO   W.EM 62

O7
−480   CORNETO   P.P.10

IVY ON ROCKS
MMIIIb   KNOSSOS
EPM II 479

MMIII
HAGIA TRIADA
BAK 67

MMIII
HAGIA TRIADA BAK.68

P2

P3
MMIII MOCHLOS, SM 31

P5
LH.II
KORAKOU   BK.53
=LAHUN, MAKET. 1450

P6
−1350   ALIKI, ATTICA   FLM XVIII

MMIII
KNOSSOS EPM 249

P4
MMII MYKENAE RAPIER EPM.II, 288

P7
LMIa   MYKENAE
TOMB VI   FLT. XI

P8
+200?
MAYENCE
E.G 5797

Q1
−600?
CERVETRI   SEDIA CORSINI
M.A.1916, 458, t.l

Q2
−600
CERVETRI SEDIA CORSINI
M.A.1916, 458

Q4
−500? BOLOGNA, STELE. M.A.1910, 594

Q3
S.APULIA   M.A.XXVI 9

Q5
−250 N.APULIA, CANOSA. RMI. 46

Q6
−250 N.APULIA. CANOSA. RMI, 46

P9
−200? ARCEVIA, NrANCONA. BRONZE VASE.   MA.1909, 694

Q7
ITALY   MIRROR DA 519

Q8
−250   N.APULIA CANOSA RMI. 46

Q9
+150? LIRIA, VALENCIA   JI 1922 I
WITH
HERAKLES
SUBJECTS

R1
LM II   PYLOS   MAIA.1909, 308

R2
R3
LM II
KNOSSOS
TAP. II 56
MM II
MA XIV
XLII

R7
UNIT
OF COLLAR
PHAESTOS
MA.1904, 614

R8
1400
IALYSOS
FLM: I

R9
−450 TODI BRONZE
MA.1916, 851

R4
KNOSSOS B.O. III 2. MS. 66

R5
EM III

R6
EM III GOURNIA
EPM 80

S6

S8

S3
+50
SIYA GATE   BSA.6, III 340

S4
+220 To 241 CHINA   SAC XII

S4
+506 TRIPTYCH
AREOBINDUS
DCD XV

COPTIC
MOSCOW G.C. LXIV, 5

T7 +528 CHINA, PILLAR. SGLC LXXXV

U1 +50 SIYA GATE   B.S.A.6.III 342

U2 BAWYT   G.C

T1 III DYN MEYDUM SENEFRU P.W.M XX

U3 GERANIUM, NATURAL   FP

U4 +500 OXYRHYNKHOS PT C XLVII

U5 +540 DIPTYCH JUSTINUS DCD XXXIV EARLIEST PERSIAN

U9

U6 +525 CONSULAR DIPTYCH DCD XLII

U7 +525 DIPTYCH PHILOXENUS DCD XXX

U8 +620 TAQI BUSTAN. SP. XCII ADAPTED FROM SUSA PALMETTO FA8

+620 TAQI BUSTAN SP. XC. PERSIAN FOLIAGE SEE LXXXVI

V1 +650 OR 750 S. MARIA ANTIQUA ROME F.P.

FOLIAGE CHANGED TO SKIRL, PU6

V5 +789 MILAN, S. AMBROGIO

V2 +825 SCHEME OF S. SABINA BELOW SCHEME OF SKIRL FOLIAGE V3

V3 +825 ROME S. SABINA

V4 F.P. +827 ROME S. GIORGIO VEL.

V6 BACK OF CROSS

V7

+800 BUDRIO   CAST IN BOLOGNA. BY BP. VITALIS +789-814

V8 +840 CROSS OF LUDOVICUS + LOTHARIUS, BOLOGNA SKIRL BROKEN LOOSE

V9 PETALS GROUPED TO SKIRL BOLOGNA REUSED IN FOSCHERARI TOMB.

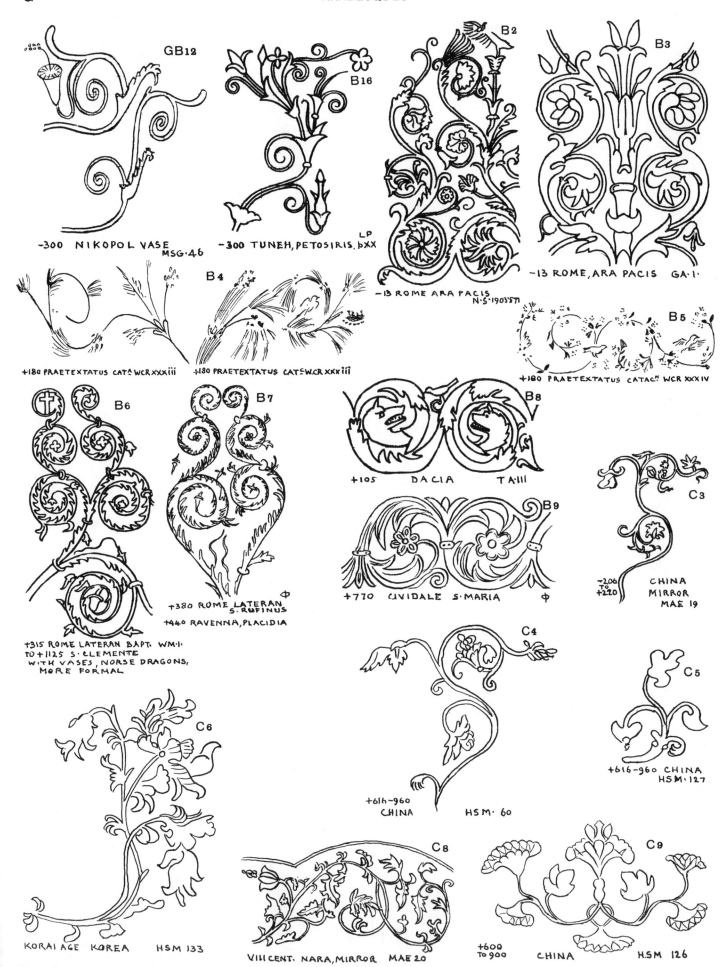

GB12
-300 NIKOPOL VASE MSG·46

B16
-300 TUNEH, PETOSIRIS, bXX LP

B2
-13 ROME ARA PACIS N·S·1903·571

B3
-13 ROME, ARA PACIS GA·I·

B4
+180 PRAETEXTATUS CAT° WCR XXXiii
+180 PRAETEXTATUS CATS·W.CR XXXiii

B5
+180 PRAETEXTATUS CATAC° WCR XXXIV

B6
B7
+380 ROME LATERAN S·RUFINUS
+440 RAVENNA, PLACIDIA
+315 ROME LATERAN BAPT· WM·I· TO +1125 S·CLEMENTE WITH VASES, NORSE DRAGONS, MORE FORMAL

B8
+105 DACIA T A·III

B9
+770 CIVIDALE S·MARIA

C3
-206 TO +220 CHINA MIRROR MAE 19

C4
+616-960 CHINA HSM· 60

C5
+616-960 CHINA HSM·127

C6
KORAI AGE KOREA HSM 133

C8
VIII CENT· NARA, MIRROR MAE 20

C9
+600 TO 900 CHINA H.S.M 126

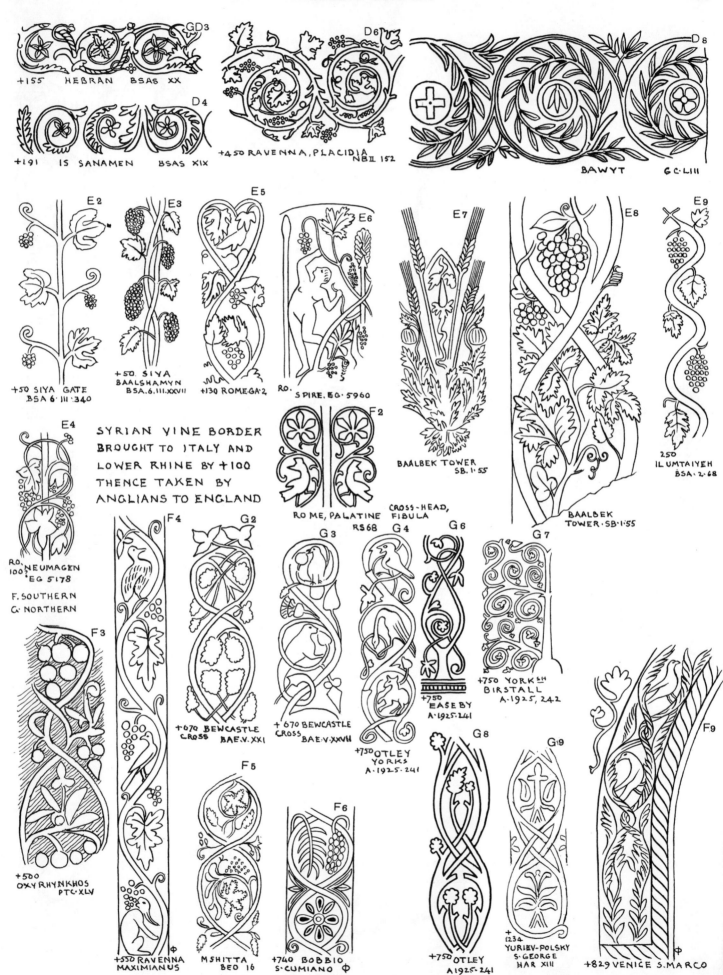

GD3
+155 HEBRAN BSAS XX

D4
+191 IS SANAMEN BSAS XIX

D6
+450 RAVENNA, PLACIDIA NB II 152

D8
BAWYT   GC·LIII

E2
+50 SIYA GATE BSA 6·III·340

E3
+50. SIYA BAALSHAMYN BSA.6.III.XXVII

E5
+130 ROME·GA·2

E6
RO. SPIRE. EG. 5960

E7

E8

E9
250 IL UMTAIYEH BSA·2·68

E4
RO. NEUMAGEN 100. EG 5178

F. SOUTHERN
G. NORTHERN

SYRIAN VINE BORDER
BROUGHT TO ITALY AND
LOWER RHINE BY +100
THENCE TAKEN BY
ANGLIANS TO ENGLAND

F2
ROME, PALATINE

BAALBEK TOWER SB. I. 55

BAALBEK TOWER · SB· I· 55

CROSS-HEAD, FIBULA RS 68

F3
+500 OXYRHYNKHOS PTC·XLV

F4
+670 BEWCASTLE CROSS BAE.V.XXI

G2

G3
+670 BEWCASTLE CROSS BAE.V.XXVII

G4
+750 OTLEY YORKS A·1925·241

G6
+750 EASEBY A·1925·241

G7
+750 YORKSH BIRSTALL A·1925·242

F5
+550 RAVENNA MAXIMIANUS

M SHITTA BEO 16

F6
+740 BOBBIO S·CUMIANO Φ

G8
+750 OTLEY A 1925·241

G19
+1234 YURIEV-POLSKY S·GEORGE HAR XIII

F9
+829 VENICE S.MARCO

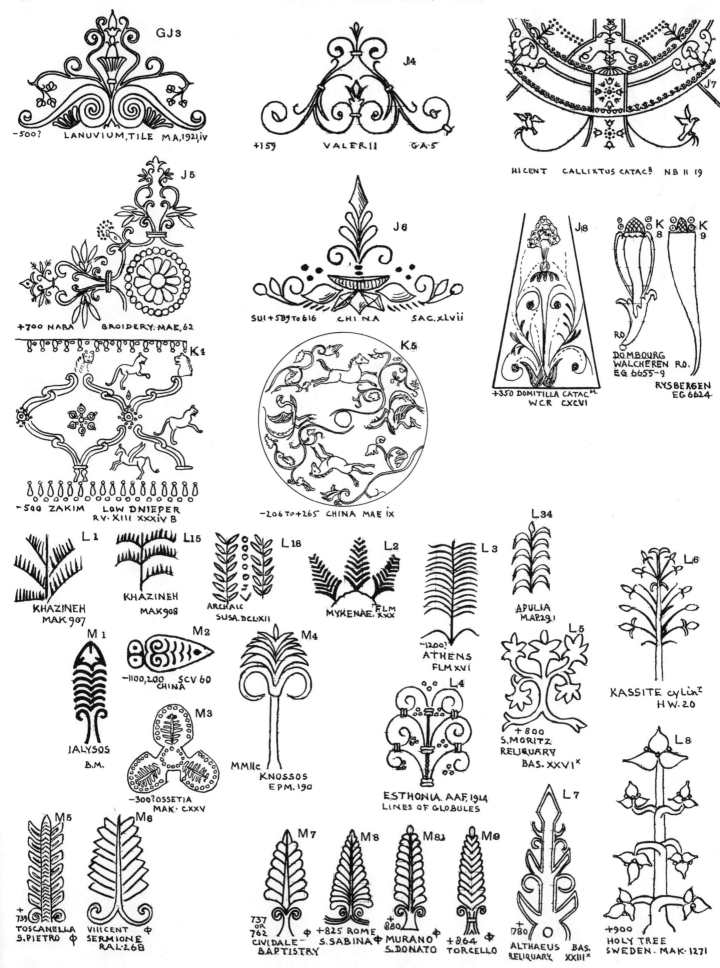

GJ3
-500?   LANUVIUM, TILE MA, 1921, iv

J4
+159   VALERII   G·A·5

J7
HI CENT   CALLIXTUS CATAC⁵   NB II 19

J5
+700 NARA   BROIDERY MAE, 62

J6
SUI +589 to 616   CHINA   SAC. XLVII

J18
+350 DOMITILLA CATAC^M.   WCR CXCVI

K8 K9
RD.
DOMBOURG WALCHEREN RD. EG 6655-9
RYSBERGEN EG 6624.

K1
-500 ZAKIM   LOW DNIEPER   RV. XIII XXXIV B

K5
-206 to +265 CHINA MAE ix

L1
KHAZINEH MAK 907

L15
KHAZINEH MAK 908

L18
ARCHAIC SUSA. DCLXII

L2
MYKENAE XXX   FLM

L3
-1200? ATHENS FLM XVI

L34
APULIA M.AP.29.1

L6
KASSITE cylin² HW. 20

M1
IALYSOS B.M.

M2
-1100, 200   SCV 60 CHINA

M3
-300? OSSETIA MAK. CXXV

M4
MMII c
KNOSSOS EPM. 190

L4
ESTHONIA. AAF, 1914 LINES OF GLOBULES

L5
+800 S.MORITZ RELIQUARY BAS. XXVI ˣ

L8

M5
+739 TOSCANELLA S.PIETRO Φ

M6
VIII CENT SERMIONE RAL·268

M7
737 OR 762 CIVIDALE BAPTISTRY Φ

M8
+825 ROME S.SABINA Φ

M81
+880 MURANO S.DONATO Φ

M9
+864 TORCELLO Φ

L7
+1780 ALTHAEUS RELIQUARY BAS. XXIII ˣ

+900 HOLY TREE SWEDEN. MAK. 1271

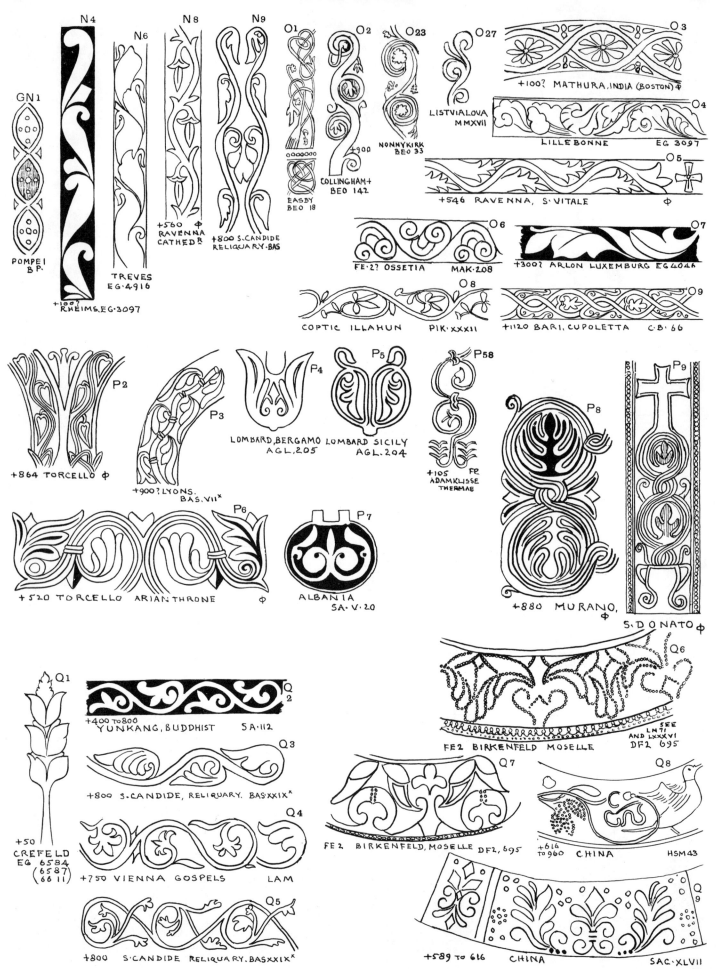

GN1
POMPEI B.P.

N4
+100?
RHEIMS. EG·3097

N6
TREVES
EG·4916

N8
+560
RAVENNA CATHED.R

N9
+800 S.CANDIDE
RELIQUARY·BAS

O1
EASBY
BEO 18

+900
COLLINGHAM+
BEO 142

O2

O23
NONNYKIRK
BEO 33

O27
LISTVIALOVA
MMXVII

+100? MATHURA, INDIA (BOSTON)
O3

LILLEBONNE
O4
EG 3097

+546 RAVENNA, S·VITALE
O5

FE·2? OSSETIA   MAK·208
O6

+300? ARLON LUXEMBURG EG·404A
O7

COPTIC ILLAHUN   PIK·XXXII
O8

+1120 BARI, CUPOLETTA   C·B·66
O9

P2
+864 TORCELLO

P3
+900? LYONS.
BAS·VII

P4
LOMBARD, BERGAMO
AGL.205

P5
LOMBARD SICILY
AGL.204

P58
+105 FR·
ADAMKLISSE
THERMAE

P8
+880 MURANO,

P9
S·DONATO

P6
+520 TORCELLO ARIAN·THRONE

P7
ALBANIA
SA·V·20

Q1
+50
CREFELD
EG 6584
(6587)
(6611)

Q2
+400 TO 800
YUNKANG, BUDDHIST   SA·112

Q3
+800 S·CANDIDE, RELIQUARY. BAS·XXIX

Q4
+750 VIENNA GOSPELS   LAM

Q5
+800   S·CANDIDE RELIQUARY. BAS·XXIX

Q6
FE2 BIRKENFELD MOSELLE
SEE
LN 71
AND LXXXVI
DF2 695

Q7
FE2   BIRKENFELD, MOSELLE DF2, 695

Q8
+616
TO 960   CHINA   HSM43

Q9
+589 TO 616   CHINA   SAC·XLVII

S2 — MMHI MYKENAE GR.IV SS.238

S4 — -700? IALYSOS PITHOI SAA 1926·222

S5 — -700? IALYSOS SAA·1926·209

S6 — LMII ZYGOURIES BZ·129

S7 — -1200 TRIPOLYEA MSG·30 KIEV

S8 — LMII·ISOPATA· TDA 64

S9 — LMII·ISOPATA·TDA 64

T2 — S.APULIA MA XXVIII·1

T3 — LM·I JHS 1903·3

T6 — FALERII M I·321·10

T7 — CAPPADOCIA GCC·1658,31B

T8 — MYKENAE FLM·XXVII

U1 — +60 VITALIS, POMPEII JRS·1914·V

U2 — +470 CONSULAR DIPTYCH DCD XXXVIII

U3 — +800 S.MORITZ. RELIQUARY BAS XXV x

U4 — -250 CANOSA, N.APULIA RMI·pl 46

U45 — S.APULIA M·A·XXVIII·6

U5 — -250 CANOSA N.APULIA RMI·pl 46

U14 — +60 POMPEII JRS·1914,VIII

U8 — -300 SCYTHIAN FRONT R·I·G

U6 — +200 COTTAEUM JRS·1925,XXIII

U66 — +50 SIYA BSA·6,340

U7 — +580 ALFRISTON A·A·S·300

U9 — CHINA MAE·49

V1 — ARCHAIC TELL LO DCL·I·9

V3 — -3500UR

V2 — -1150? CRETE MA·1889,230,ii

V3 — VULCI M·I·260·6

V4 — PALAEKASTRO LM·MA·1904,571 LMIII·AJA·1941·VI ERGANOS, CRETE

V5 — MYKENAE GRAVE IV Φ

V6 — +100? MATHURA, INDIA (BOSTON) Φ

V7 — +250 VASE, EGYPT. P.E.XXXIII

V56 — BEFORE -3500 UR

V9 — +440 RAVENNA GALLA PLACIDIA Φ

V8 — TENE HELMET, BERRU M·F·S SEE E56

+616 to 960   CHINA   HSM 58

+450   HASLINGFIELD, CAMBS. A·A·S·17

-206 to +25   CHINA   SAC·XX

+220 to 41 CHINA SAC XIII

+220 to 241   CHINA   SAC XI

+600 (SUI or TANG)   CHINA   SEE LR8   HS M.108

+265 to 300   CHINA   SAC XLII

+589 to 616   CHINA   SAC XLV

GOTHIC
RECESVINTH
CLUNY. OTP. II, II

TARQUINII
MKE 204

MMIIa KNOSSOS
KAMARES WARE
EPM iii

+500 HONAN
SSC XCIII

+700?   QASR HARANEH   JSA III 15

LM·I· PALAIKASTRO
ABS. 1905, 276

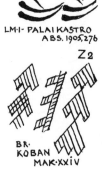

BR.
KOBAN
MAK·XXIV

BRONZE AXE
KOBAN
MAK 25

PETROSSA
COLLAR OTP. II·74

+546 RAVENNA
S. VITALE

-700?   CUMA
MA, 1913, XLII

POMPEII   B.P.

FE.1
GRANDATE
COMO BC.56

HALLSTATT
B.C. 54

+1050 S. CLEMENTE, ROME. BENO, Φ

MM II   KNOSSOS EPM, 186

+825
ROME, S. SABINA   Φ

+200?   BAIA   MA. 1922, 138

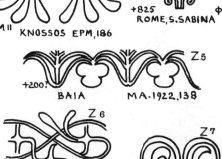

MM II KNOSSOS, EPM 186

MM I, KNOSSOS
EPM, 186

+752   Φ
CIVIDALE
CROSS OF
PELTRUDIS.

HA1

A8

-570
NAUKRT
JHS 1924 XI

BABYLONIA
J.C.B.LIII

4

B3

TELL LO, DCL.I,14

B4

ARCHAIC
TELL LO   DCL.I.10

B6

ARCHAIC, SUSA, DCL.XVIII-17

B8

CAPPADOCIA
GCC I 9810

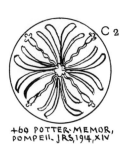

C2

+60 POTTER·MEMOR,
POMPEII. JRS.1914, XIV

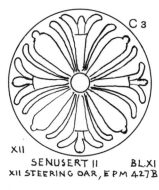

C3

XII

SENUSERT II   BL.XI
XII STEERING OAR, EPM 427B

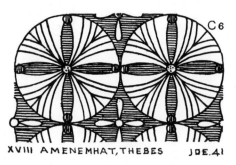

C6

XVIII AMENEMHAT, THEBES   JDE.41

C9

-600?
GELA
MA.1906, 635

D2

MYKENAE
FLM XXVIII

D4

-600
NAUKRATIS
P.NK·IV

D5

-350 PIKERMI ATTICA
RELIEF MAIA,1924,12

D6

WOODCHESTER
L.W. VII

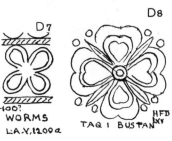

D7

+100?
WORMS
L.A.V,1209a

D8

TAQ I BUSTAN   HFD XV

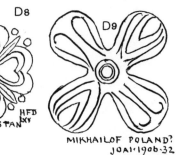

D9

MIKHAILOF POLAND?
JOAI·1906·32

5

E3

XVIII AMARNA
P.A.XVIII

E4

LM III

ABS.1903,318,17

E6

-730
NIMRUD
BELT,
LN.XXVI

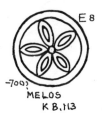

E8

-700?
MELOS
K B,113

6

F4

ARCHAIC,SUSA
DCL,XVI,21

F6

CRETE   M.S.III

F9

-570
NAUKRATIS
JHS·1924·XI

7

G1

-570
NAUKRATIS
JHS·1924·XI

G4

+600
NOCERA
MA.1918,243

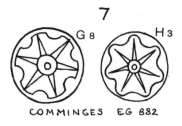

G6

+600
NOCERA, N DISK
MA 1918 343

G8

COMMINGES

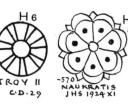

H3

EG 882

H4

XVIII AMARNA
P.A.XVIII

H6

TROY II
C·D·29

H8

-570
NAUKRATIS
JHS 1924 XI

H9

SASSANIAN HFD LXV
E.TURKESTAN

8

J1

MM I
PORTI
X.M.VIII

J3

MM II KNOSSOS, EPM,194

J4

MM III
MOCHLOS, SM 35

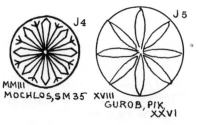

J5

XVIII
GUROB, PIK
XXVI

J6

CRETE, HS,25

J8

RELIEF
ASHUR
ACA, p·9

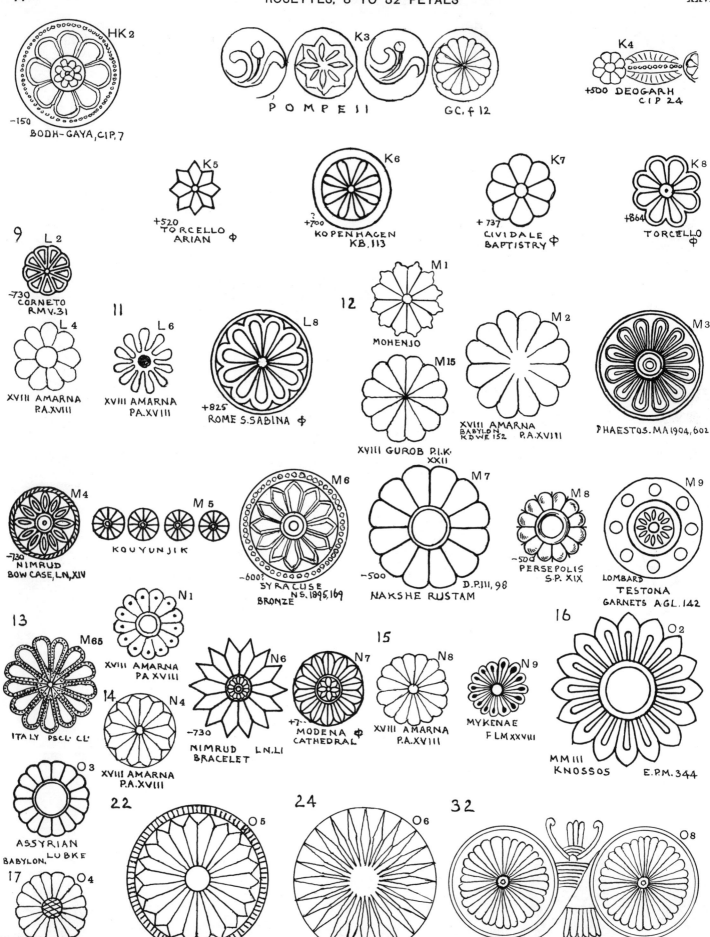

HK2
-150 BODH-GAYA, CIP, 7

K3
POMPEII
GC. f 12

K4
+500 DEOGARH
CIP 24

K5
+520 TORCELLO
ARIAN Φ

K6
? +700 KOPENHAGEN
KB. 113

K7
+737 CIVIDALE
BAPTISTRY Φ

K8
+864 TORCELLO
Φ

9 L2
-730 CORNETO
RMV. 31

L4
XVIII AMARNA
P.A. XVIII

11 L6
XVIII AMARNA
P.A. XVIII

L8
+825 ROME S.SABINA Φ

12 M1
MOHENJO

M15
XVIII GUROB P.I.K.
XXII

M2
XVIII AMARNA
BABYLON
KDWE 152 P.A. XVIII

M3
PHAESTOS. MA 1904, 602

M4
-730 NIMRUD
BOW CASE, LN, XIV

M5
KOUYUNJIK

M6
-600? SYRACUSE
N.S. 1895, 169
BRONZE

M7
-500 NAKSHE RUSTAM
D.P. III, 98

M8
-500 PERSEPOLIS
S.P. XIX

M9
LOMBARD
TESTONA
GARNETS A.GL. 142

13 M65
ITALY PSCL· CL·

N1
XVIII AMARNA
PA XVIII

14 N4
XVIII AMARNA
P.A. XVIII

N6
-730 NIMRUD
BRACELET LN.LI

15 N7
+7·· MODENA Φ
CATHEDRAL

N8
XVIII AMARNA
P.A. XVIII

N9
MYKENAE
F LM XXVIII

16 O2
MM III
KNOSSOS E.P.M. 344

O3
ASSYRIAN
BABYLON. LUBKE

17 O4
XVIII AMARNA
P.A. XVIII

22 O5
LM II BAK 312
MYKENAE TOMB 3

24 O6
MM II
PHAESTOS, EPM, 198

32 O8
-750 FALERII
M·I· 326·7

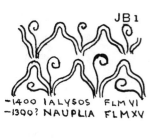

JB 1
-1400 IALYSOS FLM VI
-1300? NAUPLIA FLM XV

B 3

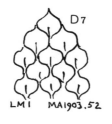

B 5
-1400? IALYSOS, SAA 1926 f 87

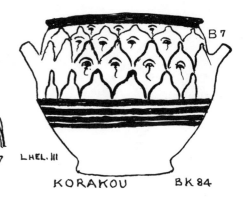

B 7

KORAKOU   BK 84

D 2
MYKENAE, FLM XXXII   CRETE   FLM p. 23

D 4
1400 IALYSOS FLM VIII

D 6
ALYABAD, MAK 912

D 5
SUSA II   CA. 15

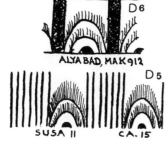

D 7
LM I   MA 1903.52

D 8
DAUNIA MA P. XIII, II

D 9
-1450 IALYSOS, SAA, 1926 f 51

G 2
-650
BISENZIO   MA. 1912, 409
PALESTRINA MA 1905, 558
VULCI   DF 380

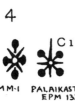

G 3
GOLD RELIEF ON
SILVER GROUND
+? EGYPT UC

G 4
FEI
TUNISIA
DF 383

G 6
LM. I. MOCHLOS
SM XI

G 8
-570 DEFENNEH, P. D. XXVII

3   KB

MMIII   57
KNOSSOS, ABS 1903

4

MM. I   C 1
PALAIKASTRO
EPM 133

C 3

C 4
PALAIKASTRO
ABS 1902, XIX

C 5
-700
CUMA
M. A. 1913 XLVII

C 6
-650 EPHESOS
BASIS
HEE VI II, 14

C 7
-570
NAUKRATIS
JHS. 1924 XI

C 8
SYRACUSE
MA 1918, 537

XVIII HAPUSENB   J DE. 40

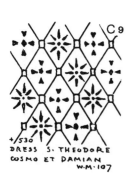

C 9
+/530
DRESS S. THEODORE
COSMO ET DAMIAN
W. M. 107

6

D 1
GOURNIA, BHG 28

D 3
-550?
OLBIA   JI. 1914, 243

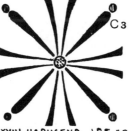

D 5
-500   ESTE   R. M. I. 7.7
BENVENUTE SITULA
MMIII KNOSSOS ABS 1903 82

D 7
+1000
STROGANOFF
IVORY WSA XXVI

D 9
+570
FAIRFORD AAS 28

7

E 2
CRETE MS. XV

E 4
-700?
CUMA
M. A. 1913 XLI

E 5
ITALY   PSCL. CLXXXVI

E 6
MONT. IV
U. P. BAVARIA, SAK. 127

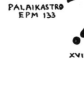

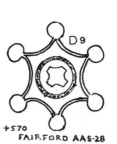

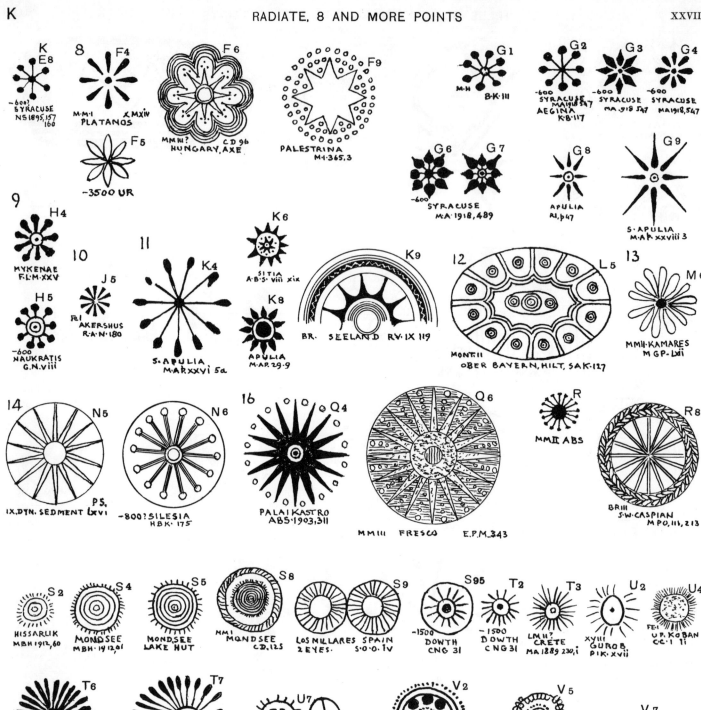

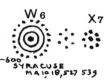

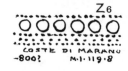

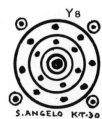

LA3
HONAN   CA·13

A8
AZILIAN ARUDY An.1904 p.145
12 M·S·OF PAU, PYRENEES
TROY 5·1·

A13
SD 31-3 AMRAH
EGYPT MADP iii

A18
SD 40 NAQADEH
P N B XXXIV. 33 d

A26

A23
NEO² FLOMBORN L.A.V·i

A28
NEO² ILBENSTADT·LA·V·i

A33
ARCHAIC. SUSA. DCL. XVii, 14

NEO² EICHELSBACH L.A.V·i.
30 M·E·OF FRANKFORT

A36
NEO² FLOMBORN ·LA.V·i

A38
NEO² RAKHMANI, W.T. 9

A43
MM 4, VASILIKI   E P M 134

A48
RAKHMANI NEO² WT ii

A53
EM I? SESKLO RV I vii

A58
DIMINI GREECE
RAKHMANI. WT. 13
RAG.3

A63
BUKOWINA. M5,93

A72
EM I? THESSALY
LIANOKLADI RV.I ix

A73
EM. SYROS R V·VII·c LXXX

A8
A83
A86
MYKENAE FLM.XXX

A98
-50 SANCHI c·I·p·13

A88
HITTITE H·H·136
THRACE. A·AHZ,1913
347

A93
E.M·I?
SESKLO. RAG.3

A68
NEO. CU. E·GALICIA·HU·II·187

MYKENAE, F.LM.xxxi

-1500 DOWTH C.N.G·36

B6
AZILIAN p
ARUDY. An.1904 137

B14
NEOL. CAPITAINE
LE TRAVAUX

B18

B22
HASBENGAU BELGIUM
NEO. M·B·H,1912, 56

B26
EM·III MOCHLOS; SM, 19

B30
IX DYN, PS, lvii
SEDMENT

B34

B38
MM· PHAISTOS
MSAC·I· ix Φ

B46
FE
ANANINO, VIATKA
A.A.F. 467

B42
FALERII
M·1·326·4
1400 IALYSOS
F.L.M. Vii

B50
CAPPADOCIA
GCC II 7651

B10
AZILIAN ARUDY
An.1904, p.146

B54
RAISAN
A·A·F·915

B66
TENE ZLONITZ
BOHEMIA MF·9

B70
700? CUMA
M'A·1913, XLi

B74
700? IALYSOS
PITHOI, S·A·A·1926,209

B78
LENGYEL
-700? CDP 283

B82
BR· KOBAN MAK. XViii
TROY S1·1889

B86
800? CUMA
M'A 1913, XVii

B90
-600 NOCERA
M·A·1918. 164

B92
TENE III LOIRE, D·F·2, 682

CAPPADOC. G.CC.II 7651

B58
MM II
CRETE E·S·M·p,161

B62
M·M·III MOCHLOS S·M·31

B96
CAPUA   K·T·XXViii

C
B98
NEMI, TEMPLE POT? M'A·1903, 320

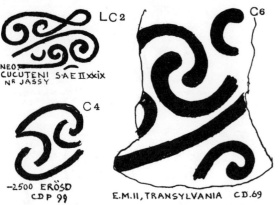

LC 2

NEO.
CUCUTENI S·AE II xxix
Nr JASSY

C6

C8

EM II TRANSYLVANIA. CD 69

C10

L·HEL·I KORAKOU   B.K.57

C 4

-2500 ERÖSD
CDP 99

E.M.II, TRANSYLVANIA   CD.69

C12

LM·I MOCHLOS, S.M·Xi

C14

CERNAVODA
SAE 8 b

C 16

NEO.CU. E.GALICIA   S·A·K· Viii, 2

C 18

NEO.CU. E.GALICIA·HU II

C 20

NEO.CU.
SERAYEVO, H.U·II, 215

C 22

-2500 ERÖSD TRANSYLV. CD.68

C 24

NEO. BUTMIR, MBH 1912

C 26

NEO. BUTMIR, MBH, 1912, 51

C 28

NEO. BUTMIR, MBH 1912, 51

C 30

NEO.CU.SERAYEVO, HU II

C 32

NEO. SERAYEVO, H.U·II·215

C 34

BUTMIR   C.A. 23

C 36

E.M. III   MOCHLOS   EPM. 76

C 48

LM·I   HAGHIA TRIADA M·A·1908, xix

C 50

LM III   TIRYNS   DCP 124

C 54

STELE III
MYKENAE
ABS 1923
130

C 38

Xii KAHUN. P.i·K·i

C 40

Xii KAHUN.P.i·K·i

HC 44

XVIII AMENEMHAT, THEBES, J·D·E 30

C 52

LM·III TRIPOLYE B., M·S·G· 32
KIEV 50 N 30 ½ E

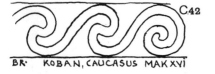

C.42

BR.   KOBAN, CAUCASUS MAK XVi

C 46

NEO.
LENGYEL
HUNGARY
RV·VII, CCi

C.43

LM·II, ALIKI, ATTICA, FLM XVIII

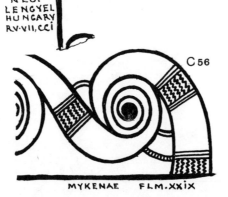

C 56

C 58

MYKENAE   FLM.XXiX

MM II. KNOSSOS EPM II iX
(AS SENUSERT II)
SEE LC 92

C 60   MM·II   UKRAINE   O·D·7·-900?

C 62   LATRONICO, LUCANIA, M·A·1916, 494

C 64   LATRONICO, LUCANIA   M·A·1916 487

C 66   MM·Ia   SEE UJ2   KNOSSOS, A·B·S·1905

C 68   BR·IV MAGLEBY DENMARK NF·I·XXI

C 70   L·M·III   TRIPOLYE A.   M·S·G·29

C 72   M·M·III   MOCHLOS   S·M·51

C 78   TOMSK, AAF, 170

C 74   MONT·V.   HANGEBEKENS SWEDEN S·A·K·XII

C 76   ~700 PLEVNA BULGARIA   TENE MARNE MF6 R·V·XIV·LIV

C 80   HITTITE   SAE II 60

C 82   700 IALYSOS PITHOI S·A·A·1926, 221

C 84   CYLINDER   U·C.

C 86   XII   U.C.

C 87   XII MMI   UC

C 88   XII MMI·   U.C.

C 89   XII MMI·   U.C.

C 90   M·M·IIIA KNOSSOS   E·P·M· 272

C 92   M·M· PHAESTOS   M.P.C. 122   SEE LC 58

C 94   BR·IV· MAGLEBY, DENMARK, NF·I·XXI

C 95   ~800?   GAURA HUNGARY   R·V· IV, XCIV

C 96   MONT·V· HANGEBEKENS SWEDEN SA·K·XII

C 98   700? IALYSOS PITHOI

C 99   S·A·A·1926, 209   ALEXANDROPOL HUGEL LOW DNEIPER R·V·XIII· XXXVI B

D 7   MMI· PLATANOS, X·M·XIII

D 35   CRETE M·S·II

D 42   LM·III IALYSOS S·A·A·1926, 81   sic

D 63   LM·II KNOSSOS TAP. II 60

D 70   TENE III MURCIA D·F·2, 685

D 84   NARCE   MA·1894, 234·

D 91   ETRUSCAN. LOUVRE, C·N·G· 60

D 14   MMI· PLATANOS, X·M·XIII

D 49   HITTITE CYL· H·W 863

D 21   MMI· KUMASA· X·M·IV

D 56   L·H·II   KORAKOU B·K· PL·V

D 77   BR   AKBUNAR, MACEDONIA, A, 1925, XXVII

D 97   2000-1500? NEW GRANGE   M·P·I·86 C·N·G· 59

D 28   CRETE, M·G·T·39

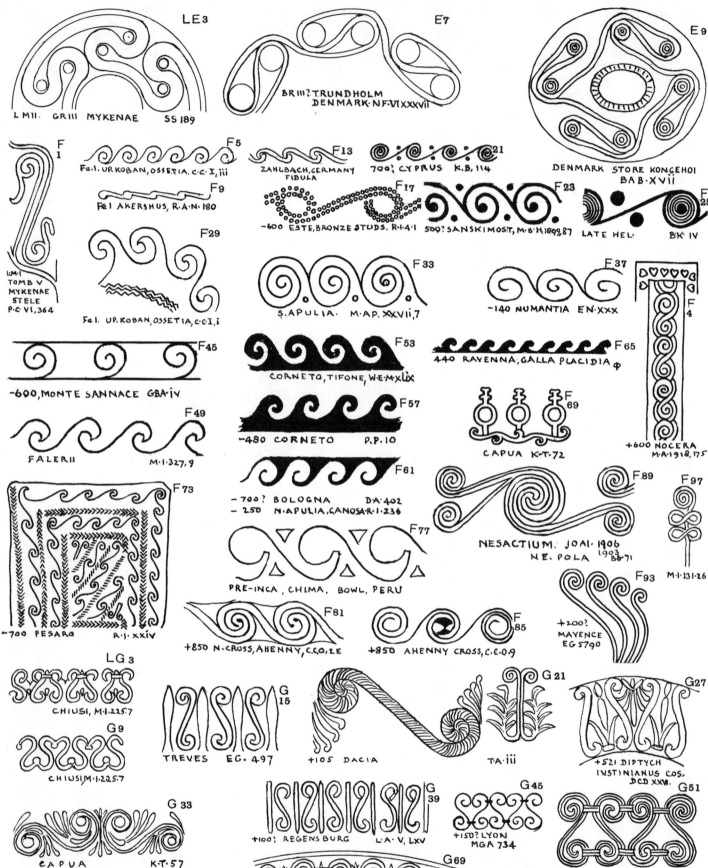

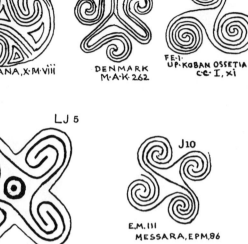

LH2
MM·I·
KALATHIANA, X·M·VIII

H3
DENMARK
M·A·K·262

H5
FE·I·
UP·KOBAN OSSETIA
C·C·I, xi

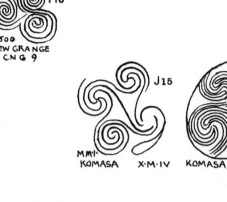

H7
TENE
MARNE   DF2.697

H8
F·E·2·
SHLESVIG-HOLSTIEN
DF2, 390
SEE C B 30

H9
FE
VLADIMIR
AAF,892

H6
~1500
NEW GRANGE
C N G 9

LJ 5
UR, SHUB-AD. FP

J10
E.M.III
MESSARA, EPM,86

J15
MM·I·
KOMASA   X·M·IV

J20
KOMASA, CRETE, X·M·IV
M.M.I

J25
MM·I·
PLATANOS, X·M·XIII

J30
MMI
PHAESTOS   M·A·1905

J35
MM·I·
KNOSSOS E·P·M·205

J40
CRETE   M·S·XIV

J45
LM·II
PYLOS MAIA 1909 285

J50
XI SA·KHENTI·KHATI   U.C.

J55
XI   EGYPT   U.C.

J60
XI-XII   U.C.

J65
MM·II· C·D·16
MYKENAE
DENMARK
BAB I

J75
TENE I. L·A·V, pl·50

J80
XVIII AMARNA P·A·XVIII

J85
MONT.V.   BAVARIA
S·A·K·127

J90
~50 SANCHI
C·I·P·13

J95
MM·I·
TROY C·D·29

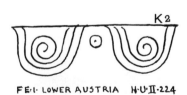

LK1
FE·I   LOWER AUSTRIA   H.U.II. 223

K4
L·M·II   MYKENAE GR·III, S·S·169

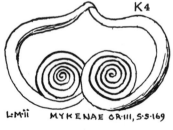

K5
MYKENAE· M·S·A·C·I·XIV

K7
MALTA D·C·P. 150

K72
MALTA, SHRINE A·LXVIII
xxxiv

K2
FE·I· LOWER AUSTRIA   H·U·II·224

K44
L·M·II   MYKENAE. GR·III·SS·170

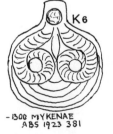

K6
~1300 MYKENAE
ABS 1923 381

K8
MM·I· XUMASA, X·M·V

K9
BR.
AKERSHUS, RAN.
1251

K3
DONETZ   C·D·86

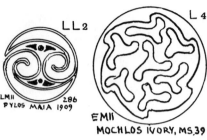

LL 2
LM II   2.86
PYLOS MAIA 1909

L 4
EM II
MOCHLOS IVORY, MS.39

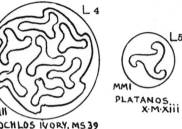

L 5
MM I
PLATANOS...
X.M.Xiii

L 7
MM I
PLATANOS...
X.M.Xiii

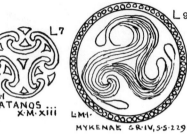

L 9
LM I
MYKENAE GR·IV, S·S·229

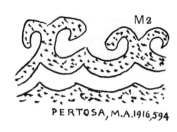

M 2
PERTOSA, M.A.1916,594

M 19
NEO· BUTMIR HBK·VI

M 20
NEO· BUTMIR·HBK·VI

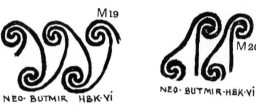

M 4
M.A 1899,583
SALERNO, CAVE

M 7
V.DYN, ASSA. U.C.

M 13
IX.DYN P.S.lvii SEDMENT

M 16
X.DYN, P.S.lvii SEDMENT

M 29
EM·III KAMARES EPM,77

M 32
EM·III CDii CRETE H.TRIADA,THOLOS

M 37
EM·II CRETE, M·S·XII

M 40
XII LAHUN P.I.K.X,144

M 43
M.M.I, XM·viii PORTI, CRETE

M 46
MM.I, XM.Xiii PLATA·NOS

M 48
XI? U.C. EGYPT

M 52
XII U.C. EGYPT

M 55
XII. P.I.K.X. 176 EGYPT

M 57
XII MMI-II, U.C EGYPT

M 64
LM II
PYLOS MAIA 1909.284

M 67
-1050 GR.V. MYKENAE S.S.145

M 68
FE.I LANGELEBARN LOWER AUSTRIA CA..20

M 73
XVIII EGYPT U.C.

M 88
CRETE AJA 1897, 259

M 79
M 82
FE.I. W.NORWAY RAN.294

M 76
-650?
EPHESOS BASIS HEE·VIII 27

M 83
M 87
-650?
EPHESOS BASIS HEE·IX 47

EPHESOS WEST HEE·IX 46

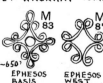

M 92
EPHESOS -650 BASIS HEE VIII 25

M 93
-650?
EPHESOS BASIS HEE·IV 31

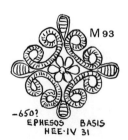

M 94
-650?
EPHESOS BASIS HEE·VIII 29

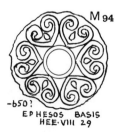

M 96
700 CRETE K.B· 114

M 97
-1800? HUNGARY CD P.270

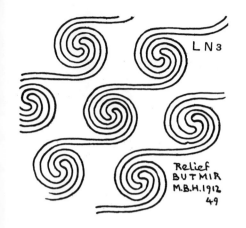

LN3

Relief
BUTMIR
M.B.H. 1912
49

N7

BUTMIR
CA 23

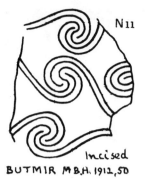

N11

Incised

BUTMIR M.B.H. 1912, 50

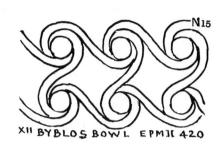

N15

XII BYBLOS BOWL EPMII 420

N19

XVIII, L·M·II AMARNA   P.A. X

N23

KAMEIROS
SINGLE LINE· ABS·1906,72

N 27

−700? IALYSOS PITHOI   S·A·A·1926, 210
SYRO·HITTITE CYLINDERS, HW855−7
−650 CRETE MAIA 1906, xxiii

N31

L·M·I   PSEIRA   B·A·K·167

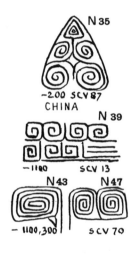

N35

−200 SCV 87
CHINA

N 39

−1100   SCV 13

N43   N47

−1100,300   SCV 70

N 51

XIX L·M·III   NESI·PA·NEFER·HETEP, J·D·E·51

N 55

L·M·II ORCHOMENOS B·A·K   206

N59

MM I·SPHOUNGARAS
MGP Lix

N 63

MM·I·SPHOUNGARAS
MGP I· Lix

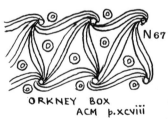

N67

ORKNEY BOX
ACM p. xcviii

N 71

−480 BIRKENFELD
R·V·VII·CXCI
SEE G Q 6,7· LXXXVII 82

N 75

FE·2· BIRKENFELD, MOSELLE DF2·695

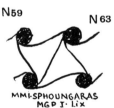

N 79

KAKOVATOS A·M·1909,xii

N83

FE·I· WALDALGESHEIM, 8·M·C·E

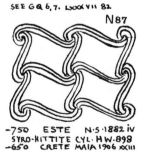

N87

−750 ESTE   N·5·1882 iv
SYRO·HITTITE CYL· H·W·898
−650 CRETE MAIA 1906 xxiii

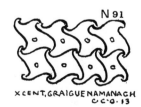

N 91

X CENT. GRAIGUE NAMANAGH
C·C·O·13

LO

GOZO, GIGANTEIA ETP. 68

THESSALY
NEO² RAKHMANI WT. i

O14

BARANYA, HUNGARY   S·A·26

O19

TARXIEN A. 1916, XXii

O24

TARXIEN, A. 1916, XVi

O29

MALTA SHRINE   φ
A·LXVIII, XXXiV

O34

MALTA, BENCH, A. LXVIII, XXXVii

O39

TARXIEN, A. 1916 XVi

O44

TARXIEN   A. 1916, XXi

O49

CRETE   MA· 1895 IX

O54

MALTA   A·LXVIII, 282

O64

MORITZING, TYROL
B.C. 77

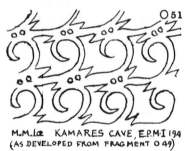

O51

M.M. Iα KAMARES CAVE, E.P.M·I 194
(AS DEVELOPED FROM FRAGMENT O 49)

O59

LM II
PYLOS MAIA, 1909, 283

O69

MALTA, BENCH, A LXVIII, XXXVii
φ

O71

DRESS, HAGHIA TRIADA MA· 1903 X

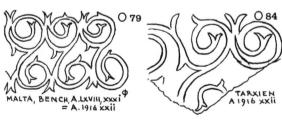

O79

MALTA, BENCH, A. LXVIII, XXXi   φ
= A. 1916 XXii

O84

TARXIEN
A 1916 XXii

O74

MALTA BOWL   A. LXVIII, 280

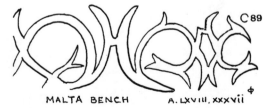

C89

MALTA BENCH   A. LXVIII, XXXVii
φ

O94

TARXIEN A. 1914 XXi

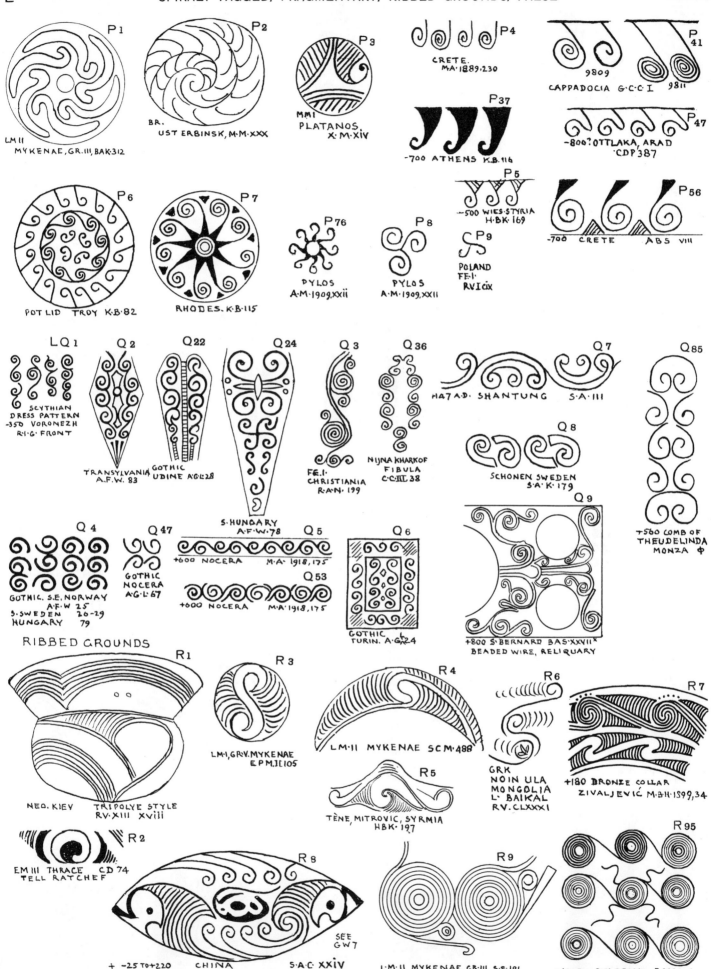

P 1   LM II   MYKENAE, GR. III, BAK. 312

P 2   BR. UST ERBINSK, M.M.XXX

P 3   MM I PLATANOS, X.M.XIV

P 4   CRETE. M.A·1889·230

P 41   9809   9811   CAPPADOCIA G·C·C·I

P 37   -700 ATHENS K.B.116

P 47   -800? OTTLAKA, ARAD CDP 387

P 6   POT LID TROY K·B·82

P 7   RHODES. K·B·115

P 76   PYLOS A·M·1909, XXII

P 8   PYLOS A·M·1909, XXII

P 9   POLAND FE·I· RV I cix

P 5   -500 WIES·STYRIA H·BK·169

P 56   -700 CRETE   A.B.S VIII

LQ 1   SCYTHIAN DRESS PATTERN -350 VORONEZH R·I·G· FRONT

Q 2   TRANSYLVANIA A.F.W. 83

Q 22   GOTHIC UDINE A·G·L·28

Q 24   S. HUNGARY A.F.W·78

Q 3   FE·I· CHRISTIANIA R·A·N· 199

Q 36   NIJNA KHARKOF FIBULA C·C·III 38

Q 7   H47 A.D. SHANTUNG   S·A·III

Q 8   SCHONEN SWEDEN S·A·K· 179

Q 85   +560 COMB OF THEUDELINDA MONZA Φ

Q 9   +800 S. BERNARD BAS.XXVII× BEADED WIRE, RELIQUARY

Q 4   GOTHIC. S.E. NORWAY A.F·W 25 S·SWEDEN 26-29 HUNGARY 79

Q 47   GOTHIC NOCERA A·G·L· 67

Q 5   +600 NOCERA   M.A· 1918, 175

Q 53   +600 NOCERA   M.A· 1918, 175

Q 6   GOTHIC TURIN. A·G·24

RIBBED GROUNDS

R 1   NEO. KIEV   TRIPOLYE STYLE RV·XIII xviii

R 3   LM·I, GR·V· MYKENAE E·P·M·II·105

R 4   LM·II MYKENAE SCM·488

R 5   TÈNE, MITROVIC, SYRMIA H·BK· 197

R 6   GRK NOIN ULA MONGOLIA L· BAIKAL RV·CLXXXI

R 7   +180 BRONZE COLLAR ZIVALJEVIC M·B·H· 1899, 34

R 2   EM III THRACE CD 74 TELL RATCHEF

R 8   + -25 TO +220   CHINA   S·A·C XXIV   SEE GW 7

R 9   LM·II MYKENAE, GR·III, S·S·191

R 95   -1000 BOLOGNA R.M.V. 4

LS

S3

MM. KYTHERA STEATITE, M·S·40
EP M II 117 B

S7

—500 NAKSHE RUSTAM DP III 92

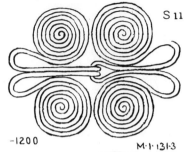

S11

—1200   M·I·131·3

S16

ZENJIRLI
SHIR·123

S19

XII? PBS vii 73
EGYPT

S27

LM II·GR·V, MYKENAE
SS 145

S31

S. CROSS
CASTLE DERMOT
C·C·O·1

S36

BR III SW. CASPIAN
M·P·O·III·213

S41

L·M·I
TOMB V MYKENAE, SS·274

S46

FRANK. VAUD, AFW·168

S56

+850 AHENNY, C·C·O·XIVA

SEE F H, I, 2

S61

HALTON OF CADBOLL SSS·XXV

S81

CAHIR LEHILLAN   C·C·O J9

S52

CLONFERT, G·C·O·3 C

S66

LINDISFARN
+700 MLG 27

S71

+924 MUIRDACH. MONASTERBOICE.   C·C·O·2 F

S91

+800 CAVAN   A·1914 xxvii

LT

T1

SYROCAPPADOC. AIDIN
DCL. XCVI, 24

T16

UP. KOBAN
OSSETIA ii
C·C·I ii

T2

PRAG   S·A·K·VIII·I

T3

SCANDINAVIAN AXE, CD 102

T4

ILKLEY
BEO 59

T5

DACRE
BEO. 42

T59

+770 ELY   A·1915, 236

T6

KINITTY CROSS   G·C·O·3 G

T7

+850 AHENNY
C·C·O·15

T8

—1350 MYKENAE
ABS 1923, 107

T9

+450 FRILFORD
A·A·S·19

T95

+450 OXON·A·A·S·18

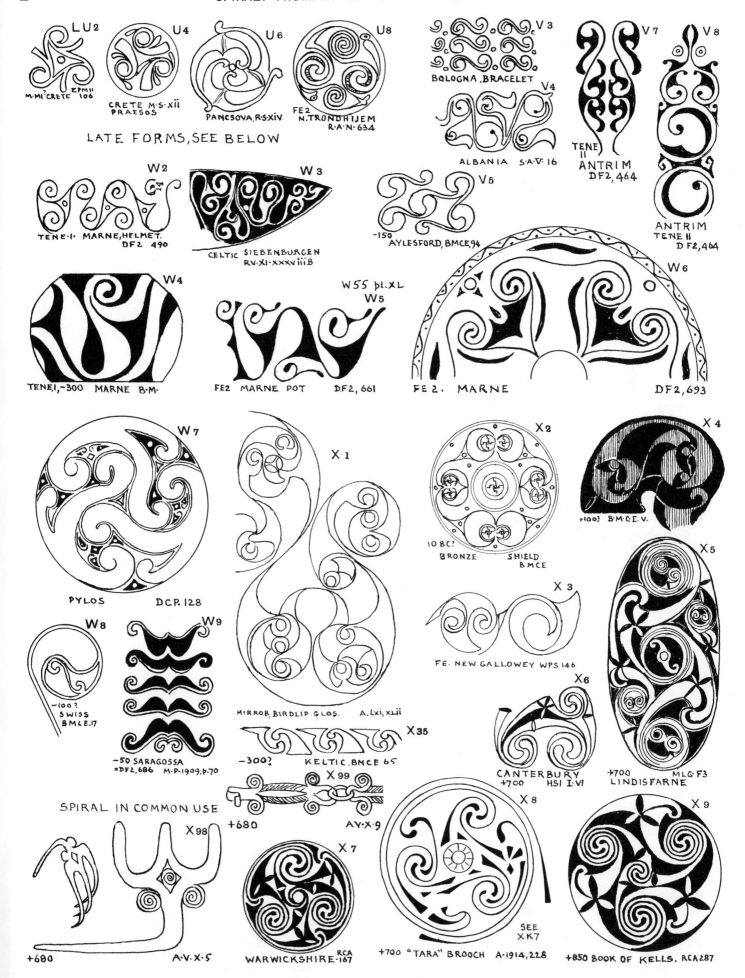

LU2 — M.MI·CRETE EPM II 106

U4 — CRETE M·S·XII PRAESOS

U6 — PANCSOVA, R·S·XIV

U8 — FE2 N·TRONDHJEM R.A·N·634

LATE FORMS, SEE BELOW

V3 — BOLOGNA, BRACELET

V4 — ALBANIA S·A·V·16

V7   V8 — TENE II ANTRIM DF2, 464

W2 — TENE·I· MARNE, HELMET. DF2 490

W3 — CELTIC SIEBENBURGEN R·V·XI·XXXViiiB

V5 — -150 AYLESFORD, BMCE 94

ANTRIM TENE II D F2, 464

W4 — TENE I, -300 MARNE B·M·

W5   W55 pl.XL — FE2 MARNE POT DF2, 661

W6 — FE2. MARNE DF2, 693

W7 — PYLOS DCP. 128

X1 — MIRROR, BIRDLIP GLOS. A. Lxi, xLii

X2 — 10 BC? BRONZE SHIELD BMCE

X4 — ·100? B·M·C·E·V.

X3 — FE. NEW GALLOWEY WPS 146

X5 — +700 MLG F3 LINDISFARNE

X6 — CANTERBURY +700 HSI I·VI

W8 — -100? SWISS BMCE.17

W9 — -50 SARAGOSSA =DF2,686 M·P·1909;p.70

X35 — -300? KELTIC. BMCE 65

X99 — +680 A·V·X·9

SPIRAL IN COMMON USE

X98 — +680 A·V·X·5

X7 — WARWICKSHIRE·167 RCA

X8 — +700 "TARA" BROOCH A·1914,228 SEE XK7

X9 — +850 BOOK OF KELLS. RCA287

Y2

FE2· NORWAY
R·A·N· 635

Y25

FE STICHEL W.P.S.121

Y3

KIRKCUDBRIGHT
BR· ARM^t· WPS·132

Y35

LINZ   MUS.
R·S· xiii,I

Y40

LINZ MUS R·S· xiii,II

Y43

LINZ MUS.
R·S· xiii I,4

Y47

KLAUSENBERG MUS.R·S·XIV,2

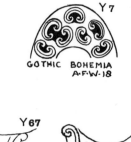

Y5

+100? IRELAND
BMCE 144

Y7

GOTHIC BOHEMIA
A·F·W·18

Y8

COPTIC CHURCH, OLD CAIRO, R·S·87

Y60

Y64

BROOCH
JSH·161.WILDE CATAL.

STOKESTOWN

Y67

WALTERS
HIST·ANC·POTT
204

Y68

+100? FAYUM PRE.LV,92

Y
90

TENE   MF·12
RHEINHESSEN

Y96

MODERN
LOUIS QUINZE

RACIAL REVIVAL
OF C BLOBS

Z2

BR. LOCHAR MOSS TORC   W.P.S ix

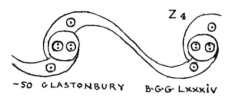

Z4

−50 GLASTONBURY   B·G·G LXXXIV

Z5

−50 GLASTONBURY.   B·G·G·Lxxiii

Z6

−50 GLASTONBURY   B·G·G·Lxxiii

Z7

+100   PORTLAND DORSET   BMCE 127

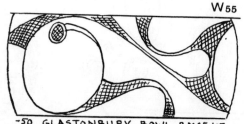

W55

−50 GLASTONBURY BOWL, BMCE,107

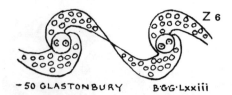

Z8

−50 GLASTONBURY   B·G·G· LXXI

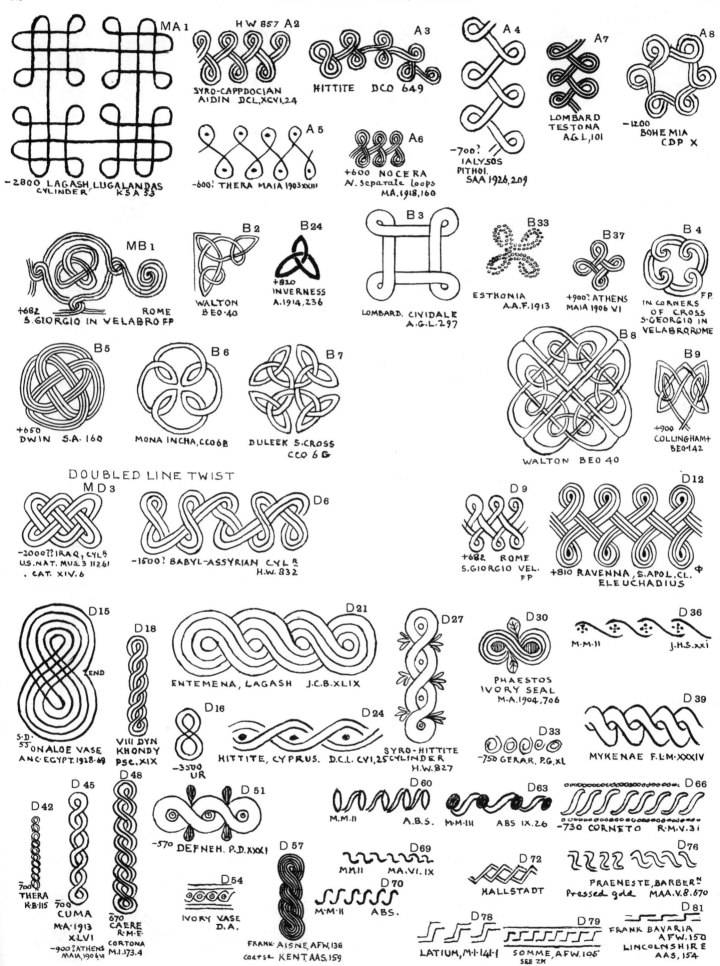

MA 1
−2800 LAGASH, LUGALANDAS
CYLINDER KSA 53

HW 857 A2
SYRO-CAPPDOCIAN
AIDIN DCL, XCVI, 24

A3
HITTITE DCO 649

A4
−700?
IALYSOS
PITHOI.
SAA 1926, 209

A7
LOMBARD
TESTONA
AGL, 101

A8
−1200
BOHEMIA
CDP X

A5
−600? THERA MAIA 1903 XXIII

A6
+600 NOCERA
N. separate loops
MA. 1918, 160

MB 1
+682 ROME
S. GIORGIO IN VELABRO FP

B 2
WALTON
BEO·40

B 24
+820
INVERNESS
A. 1914, 236

B 3
LOMBARD. CIVIDALE
A.G.L. 297

B 33
ESTHONIA
A.A.F. 1913

B 37
+900? ATHENS
MAIA 1906 VI

B 4
IN CORNERS
OF CROSS
S·GEORGIO IN
VELABROROME
F.P.

B 5
+650 DWIN S.A. 160

B 6
MONA INCHA, CCO 6 B

B 7
DULEEK S. CROSS
CCO 6 G

B 8
WALTON BEO 40

B 9
+900
COLLINGHAM+
BEO·142

DOUBLED LINE TWIST
MD 3
−2000?? IRAQ, CYLR
US. NAT. MUS. 3 112.61
. CAT. XIV. 6

D 6
−1500? BABYL-ASSYRIAN CYLR
H.W. 832

D 9
+682 ROME
S. GIORGIO VEL
FP

D 12
+810 RAVENNA, S. APOL. CL.
ELEUCHADIUS

D 15
S·D·
55 ONALOE VASE
ANC. EGYPT. 1928·69

D 18
VIII DYN
KHONDY
PSC. XIX

D 21
ENTEMENA, LAGASH J.C.B. XLIX

D 16
−3500
UR

D 24
HITTITE, CYPRUS. D.C.L. CVI, 25 CYLINDER

D 27
SYRO-HITTITE
H.W. 827

D 30
PHAESTOS
IVORY SEAL
M-A. 1904, 706

D 33
−750 GERAR. P.G. XL

D 36
M·M·II   J.H.S. xxi

D 39
MYKENAE F.L.M. XXXIV

D 42
−700?
THERA
KB·115

D 45
700 CUMA
M·A· 1913
XLVI
−900? ATHENS
MAIA, 1906 VI

D 48
670 CAERE
R·M·E·
CORTONA
M. 1. 173. 4

D 51
−570 DEFNEH. P.D. XXXI

D 54
IVORY VASE
D.A.

D 57
FRANK. AISNE, AFW, 138
COETSL KENT. AAS, 159

D 60
M·M·II   A.B.S.

D 63
M·M·III   ABS IX. 26

D 66
−730 CORNETO R·M·V· 31

D 69
M·M·II   MA.VI. IX

D 70
M·M·II   ABS.

D 72
HALLSTADT

D 76
PRAENESTE, BARBERN
Pressed gold MAA.V.8.670

D 78
LATIUM, M·I·141·1

D 79
SOMME, AFW, 105
SEE 2K

D 81
FRANK BAVARIA
AFW, 150
LINCOLNSHIRE
AAS, 154

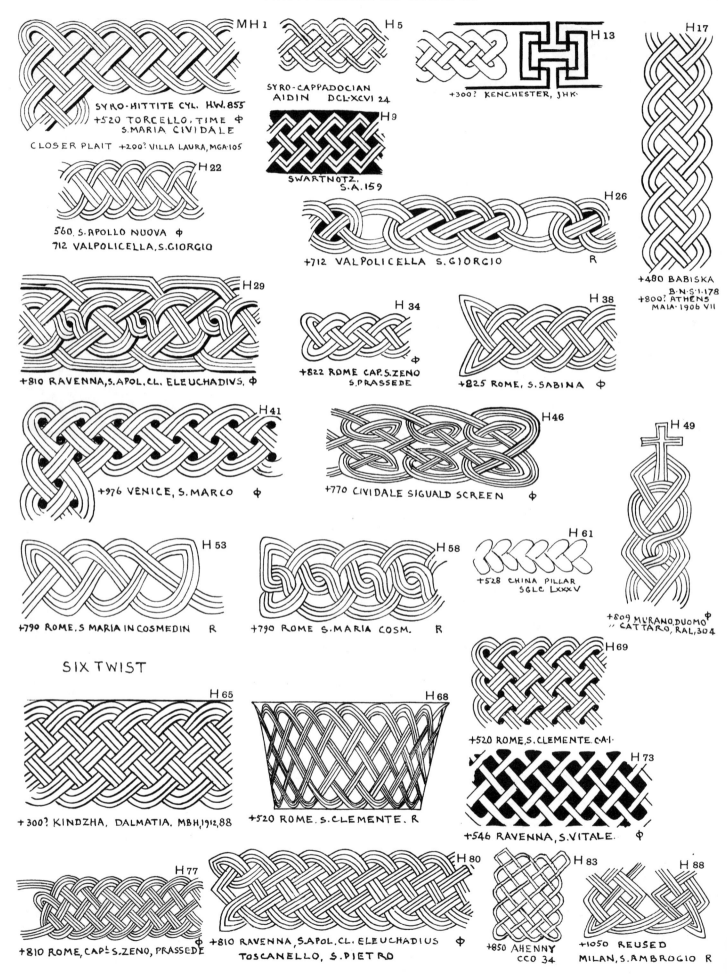

MH 1

SYRO-HITTITE CYL. H.W. 855
+520 TORCELLO, TIME Φ
S. MARIA CIVIDALE

CLOSER PLAIT +200? VILLA LAURA, MGA·105

H 5

SYRO-CAPPADOCIAN
AIDIN   DCL·XCVI 24

H 9

SWARTNOTZ.
S.A. 159

H 13

+300? KENCHESTER, JHK·

H 17

H 22

560. S. APOLLO NUOVA   Φ
712 VALPOLICELLA, S. GIORGIO

H 26

+712 VALPOLICELLA S. GIORGIO   R

+480 BABISKA
B·N·S·1·178
+800? ATHENS
MAIA·1906 VII

H 29

+810 RAVENNA, S. APOL. CL. ELEUCHADIVS. Φ

H 34

+822 ROME CAP. S. ZENO
S. PRASSEDE

H 38

+825 ROME, S. SABINA   Φ

H 41

+976 VENICE, S. MARCO   Φ

H 46

+770 CIVIDALE SIGUALD SCREEN   Φ

H 49

H 53

+790 ROME, S MARIA IN COSMEDIN   R

H 58

+790 ROME S. MARIA COSM.   R

H 61

+528 CHINA PILLAR
SGLC LXXXV

+809 MURANO, DUOMO Φ
" CATTARO, RAL, 304

SIX TWIST

H 65

+300? KINDZHA, DALMATIA. MBH, 1912, 88

H 68

+520 ROME. S. CLEMENTE. R

H 69

+520 ROME, S. CLEMENTE. C·A·I·

H 73

+546 RAVENNA, S. VITALE.   Φ

H 77

+810 ROME, CAP! S. ZENO, PRASSEDE

H 80

+810 RAVENNA, S. APOL. CL. ELEUCHADIUS   Φ
TOSCANELLO, S. PIETRO

H 83

+850 AHENNY
CCO 34

H 88

+1050 REUSED
MILAN, S. AMBROGIO R

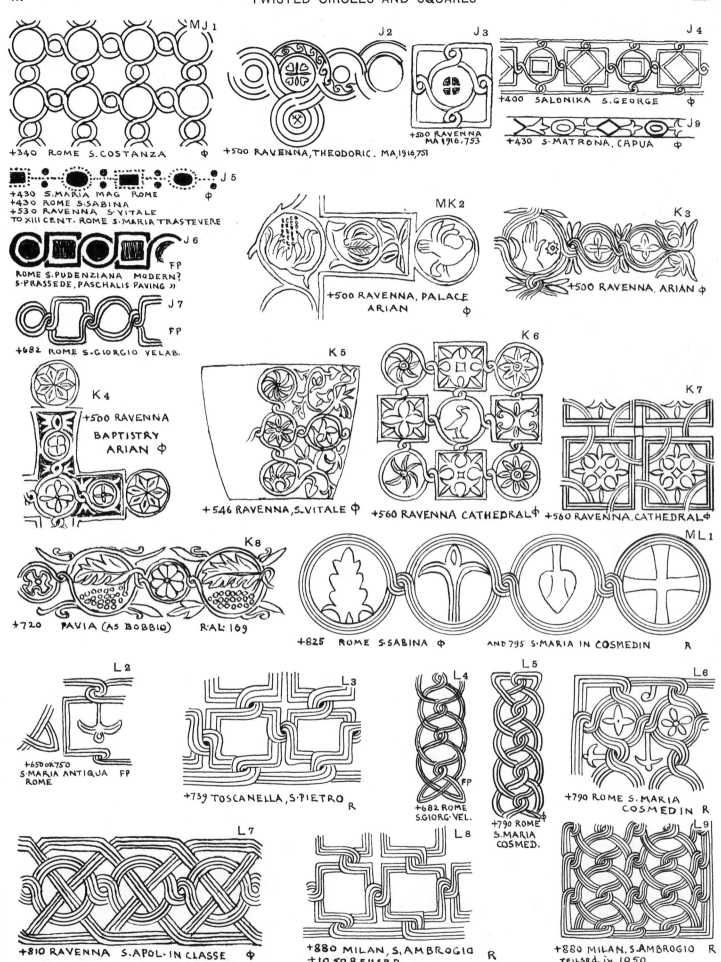

MJ.1

+340 ROME S.COSTANZA Φ

J.2

+500 RAVENNA, THEODORIC. MA,1916,751

J.3

+500 RAVENNA MA 1916. 753

J.4

+400 SALONIKA S.GEORGE Φ

J.9

+430 S.MATRONA, CAPUA Φ

J.5

+430 S.MARIA MAG ROME
+430 ROME S.SABINA
+530 RAVENNA S.VITALE
TO XIII CENT. ROME S.MARIA TRASTEVERE

J.6

ROME S.PUDENZIANA MODERN?
S.PRASSEDE, PASCHALIS PAVING »

J.7

+682 ROME S.GIORGIO VELAB.

MK.2

+500 RAVENNA, PALACE ARIAN Φ

K.3

+500 RAVENNA. ARIAN Φ

K.4

+500 RAVENNA BAPTISTRY ARIAN Φ

K.5

+546 RAVENNA, S.VITALE Φ

K.6

+560 RAVENNA CATHEDRAL Φ

K.7

+560 RAVENNA. CATHEDRAL Φ

K.8

+720 PAVIA (AS BOBBIO) R.AL.169

ML.1

+825 ROME S.SABINA Φ   AND 795 S.MARIA IN COSMEDIN   R

L.2

+650 OR 750 S.MARIA ANTIQUA FP ROME

L.3

+739 TOSCANELLA, S.PIETRO R

L.4

+682 ROME S.GIORG.VEL.

L.5

+790 ROME S.MARIA COSMED.

L.6

+790 ROME S.MARIA COSMEDIN R

L.7

+810 RAVENNA S.APOL.IN CLASSE Φ

L.8

+880 MILAN, S.AMBROGIO
+1050 REUSED R

L.9

+880 MILAN, S.AMBROGIO R
reused in 1050

MN₁ — FE2. BUSKERUD RAN·699

N 2 — FE1 STAVANGAR R·A·N· 626

N 24 — +600? SWORD ULTUNA UPSALA MCS·141

N 3 — FE2 NORWAY R·A·N· 635

N 4 — +650 NORTHUMBᴺ BINDING Φ HOBSON

N 5 — +670 BEWCASTLE B.A.E. V. XXI

N54 — +700 LINDISFARNE BAE V. XLI

N 6 — +700 CAPITAL, MLG·F11

N 66 — +700 LINDISFARNE M·L·G· F.211

N 7 — +770 CIVIDALE, BAPTISTRY, SCREEN OF SIGUALD 762-777 Φ

N 73 — 810 RAVENNA S.APOL. CL. ELEUCHAD. Φ

N 74 — 825 ROME S.SABINA Φ

N 79 — 810 RAVENNA S.AP. CL. ELEUCHAD. Φ / 840 BOLOGNA. LVDOVICVS ET LOTHARIVS CROSS. Φ

N 9 — BEALIN C.C.O. 39

MO2 — +825 ROME S.SABINA Φ

O 3 — +880 MILAN S.AMBROGIO reused 1050 R

O 4 — 880 MILAN S.AMBROGIO reused 1050 R and MONASTERBOICE MUIREDACH'S CROSS +924 Φ

O 5 — +880 MILAN S.AMBROGIO columns reused 1050 R

O 6 — MILAN, S.AMBROGIO Φ

O 7 — MILAN S.AMBROGIO R.

O 8 — 1132 PAVIA S.PIETRO AND S.MICHELE +1120 Φ

MP1   P2

TENEI ARDENNES
DF2.524

GARNETS.
LOMBARD
CIVIDALE
AGL.125
OXON, AAS,165

P4   +770 ELY   A.1915,236

P5   ILKLEY
BEO 50

P6   +900
COLLINGHAM+
BEO 142

P7   +900?
COLLINGHAM+
BEO.142

P8

Q1   +600 NOCERA UMBRA
M.A.1918,267

Q2   BERKS   AAS.23

Q3   +700 TARA BROOCH
A.1914.228

+700 LINDISFARNE
B.A.E.V,XXXIV

Q4   +700 LINDISFARNE B.A.E.V,XXXVII.

Q5   LEVISHAM   BEO 151

Q6   YORK   BEO.155

Q7   +800 WITHAM   A.1925,242

Q8   UPPLAND SWEDEN
SAK.193

Q84   +680   AV.XLI.2

Q9   +800 ST.MORITZ
RELIQUARY, B.A.S.XXV

Q94   +1000 ARDRE, GOTLAND
NSO 116

R1   HITTITE   D.C.O.649

R.4

R6   +480 BABISKA
BNS.1.178

R7   +1100?
MAUG HOLD
MANX XXXV

R3   +100? TRIER, MOSAIC.GM.19

+680 A.V.III.6

U2   +680   AV.1.4

U3   +680   AV.1.3

U4   +680   A.V.VIII,6

U5   +680   A.V.VIII.8

U6   HÄWEENMA FINLAND
AAF 1597
SIM. GETA, ALAND 1S
AAF 1723

U7   850 AHENNY N.CROSS   C.CO.5A

U8   924 MONASTERBOICE, MUIREDACH, CCO 5C

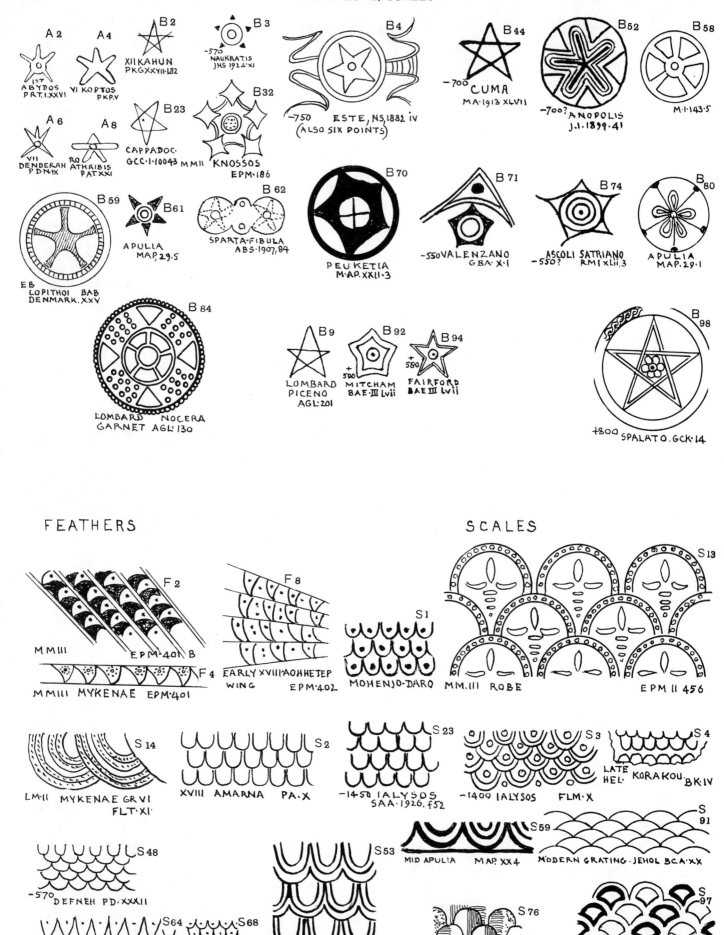

FEATHERS   SCALES

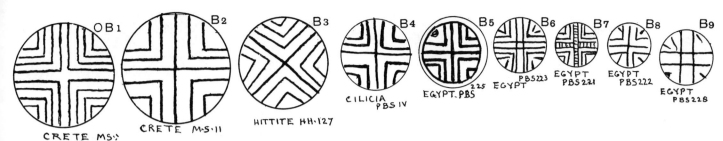

OB1 CRETE M·S·?
B2 CRETE M·S·11
B3 HITTITE HH·127
B4 CILICIA PBS IV
B5 EGYPT.PBS 225
B6 EGYPT PBS223
B7 EGYPT PBS221
B8 EGYPT PBS222
B9 EGYPT PBS228

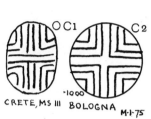
OC1 CRETE, MS III
C2 BOLOGNA M·I·75 -1000

C3 BRONZ OPEN WORK CORNETO M I·28817

C7 TARXIEN A·1916·XVIII
C8 TARXIEN A·1916 XVIII
C9 MM I PORTI XM VIII

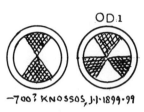
OD1 -700? KNOSSOS, J·I·1899·99

D2 -650 FEI KOBAN OSSETIA C.C. I.XXXIV

D4 N·APULIA MAP·XVIII·3

D7 INCHAGOIL CCO 8A

D8 KILFENORA CCO 8B

D9 LIVONIA AAF 2095

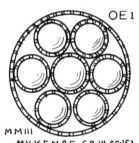
OE1 MM III MYKENAE GR·III·SS·153

E3 -1500 MC·4·12
CUMA
E4 KT·f19

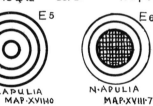
E5 N.APULIA MAP·XVII·110
E6 N·APULIA MAP·XVIII·7

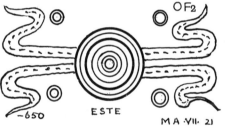
OF2 ESTE -650 M·A·VII·21

F3 -200+250 CHINA SAC VI

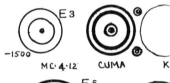
E8 MM III, PAPUDA, CRETE EPM·341

F4 NIMRUD BOTTA,XX,XV BALDRIC STUDDED LEATHER? ·LXXXIII

F7 CHINA -250 SCV, 121

E9 -700 IALYSOS PITHOI SAA 1926,210

F8 -670 CUMA R I·57

F9 KHARKOF CC·III·37

OG +340 ROME S.COSTANZA Φ
G2 GOTHIC LOMBARDY AGL 12

G5 LOMBARD TESTONA AGL·110

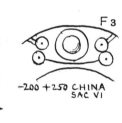
F5 -570 NAUKRATIS JHS·1924·XI

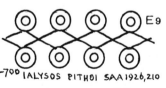
G26 +580 THEUDELINDA G C K 12

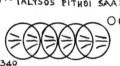
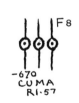

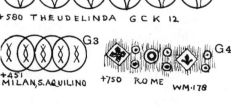

G3 +451 MILAN, S.AQUILINO
G4 +750 ROME WM·178

G6 +600 NOCERA COMB M·A·1918,285

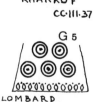
G7 +500? JAPAN RAR·1923 Ab pl.iii

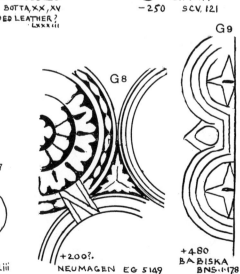
G8 +200?. NEUMAGEN EG 5149

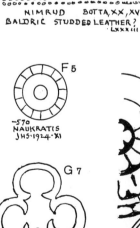
G9 +480 BABISKA BNS·I·178

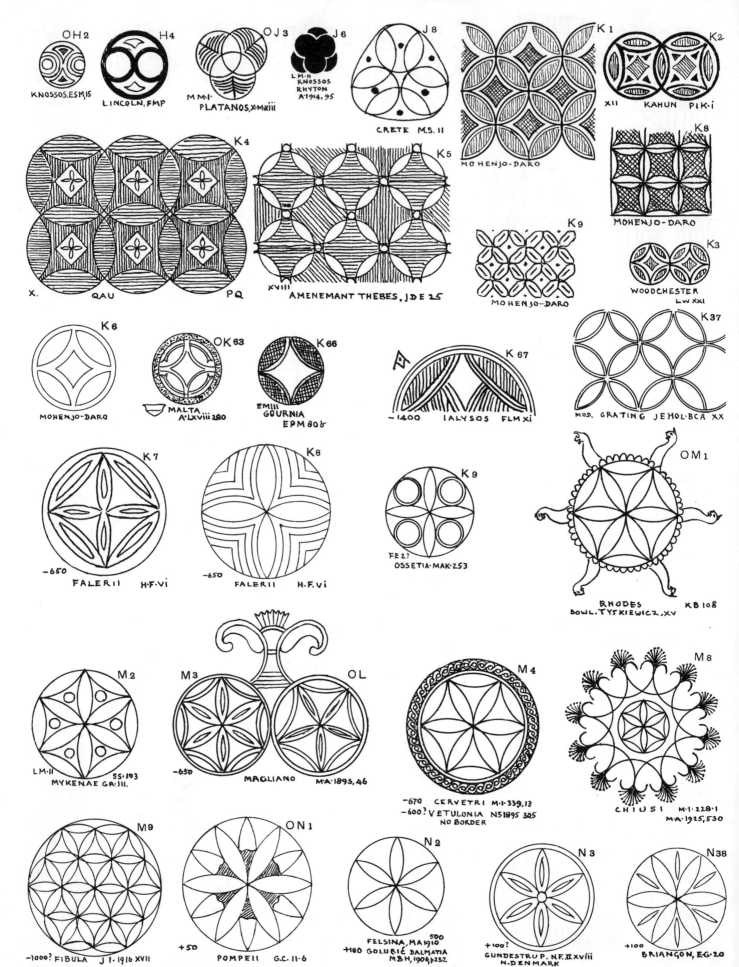

OH2 KNOSSOS.ESM15

H4 LINCOLN, FMP

OJ3 MM.I. PLATANOS. X·M·xiii

J6 LM.II KNOSSOS RHYTON A·1914, 95

J8 CRETE M.S. 11

K1 MOHENJO-DARO

K2 XII KAHUN PI·K·i

K4 X. QAU PQ

K5 XVIII AMENEMANT THEBES. J.D.E. 25

K8 MOHENJO-DARO

K9 MOHENJO-DARO

K3 WOODCHESTER LW XXI

K6 MOHENJO-DARO

OK63 MALTA A·Lxviii 280

K66 EMIII GOURNIA EPM 80b

K67 -1400 IALYSOS FLM XI

K37 MOD. GRATING JEHOL·BCA XX

K7 -650 FALERII H·F·vi

K8 -650 FALERII H·F·vi

K9 FE2? OSSETIA.MAK·253

OM1 RHODES BOWL.TYSKIEWICZ. XV KB 108

M2 LM.II 55·103 MYKENAE GR.III.

M3 -650 MAGLIANO M·A·1893, 46 OL

M4 -670 CERVETRI M·I·339,13 -600? VETULONIA N5 1895 305 NO BORDER

M8 CHIUSI M·I·228·1 M·A·1925,530

M9 -1000? FIBULA J·I·1916 XVII

ON1 +50 POMPEII G.C. 11·6

N2 500 FELSINA, MA1910 +100 GOLUBIC DALMATIA M·B·H, 1906,b232

N3 +100? GUNDESTRUP, N·F·II xviii N·DENMARK

N38 +100 BRIANÇON, E·G·20

N4

N.5

N6

N68

N7

DURA C. XCI
+1400? ASCOLI CATHED.ᴿ

COMMINGES
E.G.879

+200?
BONN E.G.6272

LOMBARD
TOSCANA
A.G.L.170

AQUILEIA N.S.1927,276

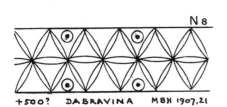

N8

N9

OO4

OO7

+500? DABRAVINA   MBH 1907,21

+850
AHENNY S·CROSS
CCO·4A

NARCE·MA·1894, 270

KHAZINEH C.ASIA
MAK 968

P
SKIRLS

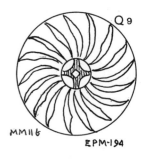

PP

PQ1

Q3

Q5

Q7

Q9

EM I–II
MOCHLOS
S M 24

CRETE, MS III

MMI   XM XIV
PLATANOS

CRETE MS III

MMI·PALAIKASTRO
A BS, 1923 SUPP XI

MM II б
EPM·194

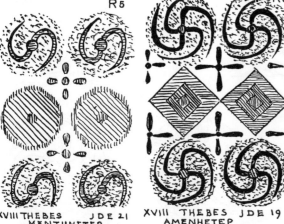

R5

R6

R7

S1

S2

S3

S4

S6

S7

S8

S9

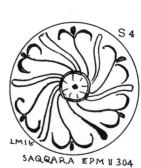

XVIII THEBES
MENTUHETEP   JDE 21

XVIII THEBES
AMENHETEP   JDE 19

XVIII THEBES NEKHT-MIN   JDE 35

–1450
SAQQARA, TETI, FG·XLII   φ

TROY
S·1·1946

TROY
S·1·1993

LM Iб
SAQQARA EPM II 304

TROY, S·1·1837

LM I·
MYKENAE GR4, SS·226

LM·I·
MYKENAE
GR 2·SS·207

LM.I.
MYKENAE GR.5· SS·257

PT3
-1100
SYRACUSE
MA 1893 t1

T6
CRETE
JHS·1927,X

T9
CHARIOT WHEEL
HITTITE, ANATOLIA
GCC·1·58

U1
-500 ANANINO
RV·T XXXVI

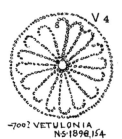

U3
-500
S·MAURO SICILY MA 1910·VI

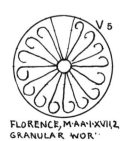

U6
-650?
IALYSOS SAA 1926·187
BEFORE
+870 S·CLEMENTE, ROME FE 2? OSSETIA MAK·CVIII
-200? KERTCH RK·XXIV

U9
-550?
IALYSOS
SAA 1926·192

V2
-700
CUMA   MA·1913,XLVII

V3
NARCE·MA 1894 288

V4
-700? VETULONIA
N·S·1898,154

V5
FLORENCE, M·AA·I·XVII,2
GRANULAR WOR'

V6
MONT IV
-750
UPPER BAVARIA SAK·129

V7
-650
FALERII HF VI

V8
-1100,200 5 CV 60
CHINA

W2
-250 ORENBURG RI·G·XXIV
PERSIAN

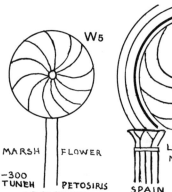

W5
MARSH | FLOWER
-300
TUNEH | PETOSIRIS
LP. PL XXXVIII

W9
L·AEMILIO
MEMMIO
SPAIN LEON

X1
-130?
AYLESFORD
BMCE 93

X2
-100
SOMME
BMCE· þl III

X3
GOTHIC AFW·23
S.E. NORWAY

X5
+500 OXYRHYNKHOS PTC·XLV

X6
+500?
KAMMUNTA
CC·III·XXI

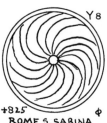

X7
NARBONNE
EG 6901,6908

X8
682 ROME
S·GIORG·VEL
SEE SY6 FP.

Y2
+650
OR
750
ROME, S·MARIA·ANT
FP

Y4
+7--
MODENA
CATHEDRAL

Y6
+770
CIVIDALE S·MARIA ɸ

Y8
+825
ROME S. SABINA ɸ
+513 CLEMENTINUS
DIPTYCH·DCD·XVI
+525 PHILOXENUS
DRESS·DCD·XXIX

Z1
+800? ATHENS
MAIA, 1906 VII

Z3
INISBOFINNE
CCO 9 F

Z5
CLONMACNOISE
CCO 9 G

Z7
RHEFERT CCO·9·1
GLENDALOCH

Z9
LOCHLEE SCOTLAND
MLW D·415

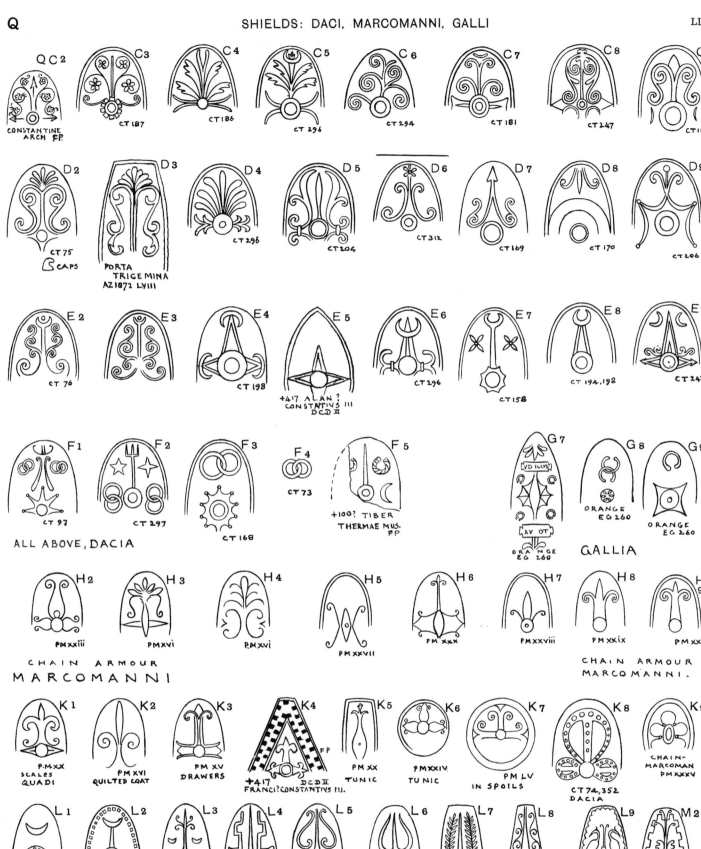

QC2 CONSTANTINE ARCH FP.
C3 CT187 · C4 CT186 · C5 CT296 · C6 CT294 · C7 CT181 · C8 CT247 · C9 CT110

D2 CT75 CAPS · D3 PORTA TRIGEMINA AZ1871 LVIII · D4 CT296 · D5 CT204 · D6 CT312 · D7 CT169 · D8 CT170 · D9 CT206

E2 CT76 · E3 · E4 CT198 · E5 +417 ALAN? CONSTANTIVS III DCD II · E6 CT296 · E7 CT158 · E8 CT194,198 · E9 CT247

F1 CT97 · F2 CT297 · F3 CT168 · F4 CT73 · F5 +100? TIBER THERMAE MUS. FP

ALL ABOVE, DACIA

G7 VD ILLVS AV OT ORANGE EG 260 · G8 ORANGE EG 260 · G9 ORANGE EG 260

GALLIA

H2 PMXXIII · H3 PMXVI · H4 PMXVI · H5 PMXXVII · H6 PM XXX · H7 PMXXVIII · H8 PMXXIX · H9 PMXX

CHAIN ARMOUR
MARCOMANNI

CHAIN ARMOUR
MARCOMANNI.

K1 P.MXX SCALES QUADI · K2 PMXVI QUILTED COAT · K3 PM XV DRAWERS · K4 +417 DCDII FRANCI? CONSTANTIVS IU. FP · K5 PM XX TUNIC · K6 P.MXXIV. TUNIC · K7 PM LV IN SPOILS · K8 CT 74,352 DACIA · K9 CHAIN-MARCOMAN PM XXXV

L1 ORANGE EG 260 · L2 NIMES EG431 · L3 ORANGE EG 260 · L4 NARBONNE EG 700 · L5 NARBONNE EG749 · L6 NARBONNE EG 692,737 · L7 NARBONNE EG 712,14,20 720,38 · L8 PROVENCE EG 46 · L9 CATIVS ORANGE EG260 · M2 ORANGE EG 260

GALLIA

M3 NARBONNE EG 712 · M4 NARBONNE EG 712 · M5 ORANGE EG 260 · M6 MAVILLY 200? EG 2067 · M7 NARBONNE EG 699 · M8 ORANGE EG 260 · M9 ARLES EG159

QP2

±0 THAMES
BMCE i

P4 CORNUFICIA
BRC I
JUNO SOSPITA
LANUVINA

P6 SHIELD
SENJERLI
-200
WAH XXIX

R2 +220? THERMAE
CARACALLA. F.R.

R3

R4 PORTA
TRIGEMINA
AZ:1872 LVIII

PORTA
TRIGEMINA
AZ:1872 LVIII

R5 DACIA
CT 73

R6 CT

R7 CT 181

R8 CT 196

R9 CT 181

T2 CAECILIA, BRC 28,30
MACEDONIAN

T3 MACEDONIAN
ROMAN

T4 SPARTA ABS

T5 ±0 ARLES EG¹27

T6 CAESAR
JULIA BRC·164

V2 +50 SENS. EG 2761

V3 +50 SENS EG 2761

V4 -50? MEAUX EG3207

V5 PORTA TRIGEMINA
AZ:1872 LVIII

V6 ±0 PROVENCE, EG 46

V7 COMMINGES

V8 EG 843

FOR SCOTTISH
SHIELDS
SEE LXXXVII QZ

X1 +200? FIBULA ENCHESTER
JRS 1925 XXXIV

X2 BERLIN   S.T.V
SCYTHIAN AND DRAGON

X3 DACIA
CT 68

X4 TERMISOS
PISIDIA
JOAI·1900,184

X5 VAISON EG295
BEZIERS 433

X6 ETRUSCAN
PERUGIA
KUE II LXXXI

X7 ETRUSCAN
PERUGIA
KUE II LXXXIV

X8 +300 FIBULA
SOMERSET
JRS,1925,230

X9 TERMISSOS
PISIDIA
JOAI·1900,185

Y1 WOODCHESTER
LW·VII

+400
RUSGUNIAS
AJA 1920 152

Y14

Y2 CU CAPRI M·A·1923,338

Y3 +150? KÖNIGSHOFFEN EG 5518

Y4 +40 SALZBURG
AJA 1920 152

Y5 +430 S.MATRONA CAPUA Φ

Y6 THEODORIC, RAVENNA
M·A·1916,750

RN1
=MM I MONDSEE
E.SWITZ? C·D 125

N3
MM III
SITEIA EPM 371
SEE ME 2

N4
L·M·II
GR·III MYKENAE, S·S·149

N5
BR·III
S·W·CASPIAN
M PO,III,213

N6
-720
HALLSTATT, A 1916,XXX

N7
-500? SANSKIMOST
M B H, 1899, 173

N8
-600 SYRACUSE, MA1918,554

N9
GOLD EARRING
ETRUSCAN, WEM·IO

RO 2
-550
OLBIA, BEADS
J1·1914 24b

O3
FE 2
BERGENNUS
R·A·N·668
SEE RQ3

O4
FE·2 BUSKERUD
R·A·N. 701

O5
FE 2. HEDEMARKEN   R·A·N,720

P 7

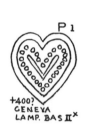

O6
WATSCH,CARNIOLA   B·C·67

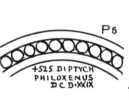

O7
-50 GLASTONBURY, BGG LXXiii

O8
-100? GLASTONBURY
POT   B.G.G.Lxxi

P 1
+400? GENEVA
LAMP. BAS II^x

P 2
BAVARIA
AFW.242

P 3
+400-700 SÖDERMANLAND
M·C·S·129

P 4
+414
KSEJBEH
B·N·S·I·170

P 5
+525 DIPTYCH
PHILOXENUS
D C D·XXIX

P 6
+462
DAR KITA   BNS·I·196

+418 DAR KITA
BNS·I·189

Q 1
MAINZ AFW,275

Q 4
LOMBARD, BRESCIA
A G L,274

Q 6
+600 TAPLOW   AAS·2

P84
+737
CIVIDALE Φ

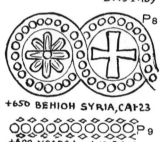
P 8
+650 BEHIOH SYRIA, CA1·23

P 9
+800 NOCERA   A·1918,210

Q 2
+650 FAVERSHAM
AAS·250

Q 5
+660
FRIESLAND
AAS·291

Q 7
+610 LANGENEHRINGEN, L·A·IV,10

Q 76
+630 RIJNSBURG, HOLLAND
AAS·223

Q 9
WURTEMBURG
A·F·W·258

Q 3
CANTERBURY, S. MARTIN, FONT
SEE RO3

Q.8
-700   A·V·XXIX,4

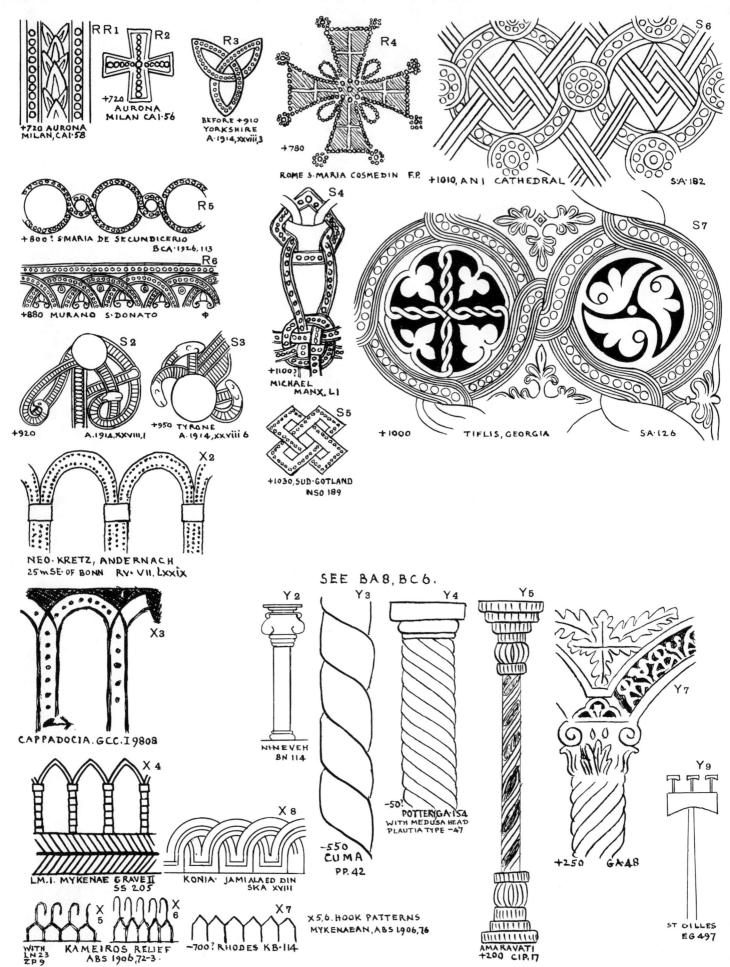

RR1

R2
+720
AURONA
MILAN CAI·56

+720 AURONA
MILAN, CAI·58

R3
BEFORE +910
YORKSHIRE
A·1914, XXVIII, 3

R4
+780
ROME S·MARIA COSMEDIN F.P.

S6
+1010, ANI CATHEDRAL
S·A·182

R5
+800? S·MARIA DE SECUNDICERIO
BCA·1926, 113

R6
+880 MURANO S·DONATO

S4
+1100?
MICHAEL
MANX·LI

S2
+920   A·1914, XXVIII, 1

S3
+950 TYRONE
A·1914, XXVIII 6

S5
+1030, SUD-GOTLAND
NSO 189

S7
+1000   TIFLIS, GEORGIA   S·A·126

X2
NEO· KRETZ, ANDERNACH
25 m SE· OF BONN   RV· VII· LXXIX

X3
CAPPADOCIA. GCC. I 9808

SEE BA8, BC6.

Y2
NINEVEH
BN 114

Y3
-550
CUMA
PP. 42

Y4
-50?
POTTERY GA·154
WITH MEDUSA HEAD
PLAUTIA TYPE -47

Y5
AMARAVATI
+200 CIP. 17

Y7
+250   GA·48

Y9
ST GILLES
EG 497

X4
LM·I· MYKENAE GRAVE II
SS 205

X8
KONIA· JAMI ALAED DIN
SKA XVIII

X5
WITH
LN 23
ZP 9

X6
KAMEIROS RELIEF
ABS 1906, 72-3·

X7
-700? RHODES KB·114

X 5,6. HOOK PATTERNS
MYKENAEAN, ABS 1906, 76

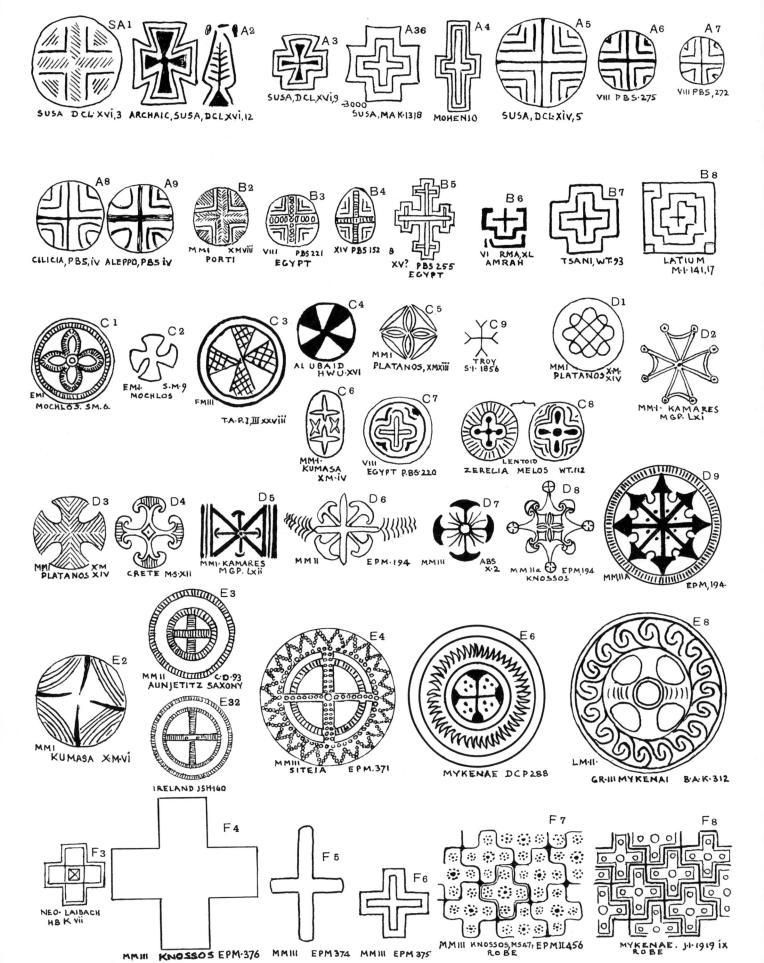

SUSA D CL XVI,3 ARCHAIC, SUSA, DCL XVI,12   SUSA, DCL XVI,9   SUSA, MA·K·1318   MOHEN1O   SUSA, DCL XiV,5   VIII PBS·275   VIII PBS,272

CILICIA, PBS, iv ALEPPO, PBS iv   MMI XMViii PORTI   VIII PBS 221 EGYPT   XIV PBS 152   XV? PBS 255 EGYPT   VI RMAXL AMRAH   TSANI, WT.93   LATIUM M·I·141,17

EMI MOCHLOS, SM·6·   EMI S·M·9 MOCHLOS   FMIII T·A·P·I,III xxviii   AL UBAID HWU·XVI   MMI PLATANOS, XMXIII   TROY S·I·1856   MMI PLATANOS XM·XIV   MM·I· KAMARES M·GP· Lxi

MM·I· KUMASA XM·iv   VIII EGYPT P·BS·220   LENTOID ZERELIA MELOS WT.112

MMI PLATANOS XM·XIV   CRETE M·S·XII   MMI· KAMARES M·GP· Lxii   MM II   E·PM·194   MMIII   ABS X·2   MM IIa EPM·194 KNOSSOS   MMIIA EPM,194

MMI KUMASA X·M·Vi   MM II C·D·93 AUNJETITZ SAXONY   IRELAND JSH160   MMIII SITEIA EPM·371   MYKENAE DCP288   LM·II· GR·III MYKENAI B·A·K·312

NEO· LAIBACH HBK Vii   MMIII KNOSSOS EPM·376   MMIII EPM374   MMIII EPM375   MMIII KNOSSOS,MSA7, EPMII·456 ROBE   MYKENAE. J·I·1919 iX ROBE

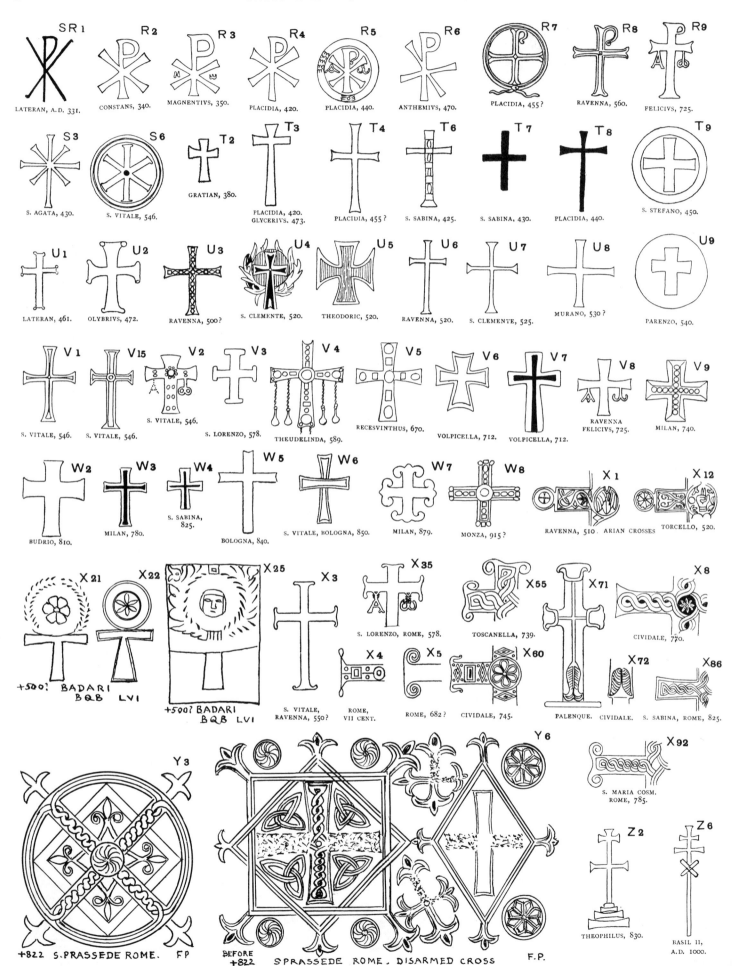

SR 1 — LATERAN, A.D. 331.
R 2 — CONSTANS, 340.
R 3 — MAGNENTIVS, 350.
R 4 — PLACIDIA, 420.
R 5 — PLACIDIA, 440.
R 6 — ANTHEMIVS, 470.
R 7 — PLACIDIA, 455?
R 8 — RAVENNA, 560.
R 9 — FELICIVS, 725.

S 3 — S. AGATA, 430.
S 6 — S. VITALE, 546.
T 2 — GRATIAN, 380.
T 3 — PLACIDIA, 420. GLYCERIVS. 473.
T 4 — PLACIDIA, 455?
T 6 — S. SABINA, 425.
T 7 — S. SABINA, 430.
T 8 — PLACIDIA, 440.
T 9 — S. STEFANO, 450.

U 1 — LATERAN, 461.
U 2 — OLYBRIVS, 472.
U 3 — RAVENNA, 500?
U 4 — S. CLEMENTE, 520.
U 5 — THEODORIC, 520.
U 6 — RAVENNA, 520.
U 7 — S. CLEMENTE, 525.
U 8 — MURANO, 530?
U 9 — PARENZO, 540.

V 1 — S. VITALE, 546.
V 15 — S. VITALE, 546.
V 2 — S. VITALE, 546.
V 3 — S. LORENZO, 578.
V 4 — THEUDELINDA, 589.
V 5 — RECESVINTHUS, 670.
V 6 — VOLPICELLA, 712.
V 7 — VOLPICELLA, 712.
V 8 — RAVENNA FELICIVS, 725.
V 9 — MILAN, 740.

W 2 — BUDRIO, 810.
W 3 — MILAN, 780.
W 4 — S. SABINA, 825.
W 5 — BOLOGNA, 840.
W 6 — S. VITALE, BOLOGNA, 850.
W 7 — MILAN, 879.
W 8 — MONZA, 915?
X 1 — RAVENNA, 510. ARIAN CROSSES
X 12 — TORCELLO, 520.

X 21 — +500? BADARI BQB LVI
X 22 — +500? BADARI BQB LVI
X 25 — +500? BADARI BQB LVI
X 3 — S. VITALE, RAVENNA, 550?
X 35 — S. LORENZO, ROME, 578.
X 4 — ROME, VII CENT.
X 5 — ROME, 682?
X 55 — TOSCANELLA, 739.
X 60 — CIVIDALE, 745.
X 71 — PALENQUE. CIVIDALE.
X 8 — CIVIDALE, 770.
X 72 — S. SABINA, ROME, 825.
X 86 — S. SABINA, ROME, 825.

X 92 — S. MARIA COSM. ROME, 785.

Y 3 — +822 S. PRASSEDE ROME. F.P.
Y 6 — BEFORE +822 S. PRASSEDE ROME. DISARMED CROSS F.P.

Z 2 — THEOPHILUS, 830.
Z 6 — BASIL II, A.D. 1000.

TJ1   EM·III BOHEMIA   C·D·81

J2   CAPPADOCIA   G·C·C·I·11

J3   S. OF PO   M·I·24·13

J4   DAUNIA   M·AP·XIV·2   LATIUM   M·I·140·9

J25   MOHENJO-DARO

J6   -750 GERAR   P.G. xLi

J7   FE.I. LANGELEBARN LOWER AUSTRIA   CA 20

J8   -800 CUMA   M·A·1913,xi

J9   -750 GERAR   P.G. xLi

K2   VOLTERRA. M·I·171·2

K3   -1200-600? BRITAIN ABA·XXIII 2,51 122,180

K5   -1200? BRITAIN ABA XXV, 121

K7   -1200? BRITAIN A·B·A·XXIII.12

K8   PORTUGAL S-00·VI

K9   -1100 GROTTAFERRATA M·I· 136

L1   -600? M·G·

L2   -800? M·G

L3   FALERII   M·A·1894,187

L4   -700? BRITAIN A·B·A·CVI,169

L5   QUERCIANELLA   M·I·169·19

L6   MID APULIA M·AP·XX·7

L8   LM·III LIANOKLADHI WT 32

L9   QUERCIANELLA   M·I·169·19

N1   LATIUM M·I·141   CORNETO M·I·277

N2   -1100,200 CHINA SCV 68

N3   MID APULIA. M·AP·XX·14

N4   N5   -570 NAUKRATIS JHS 1924,XI

N6   -600 P·NK·V

N7   600 SYRACUSE ·MA·1918,536

N8   MID APULIA   M·AP·XX·3

N9   GALLEN PRIORY G·C·O·7C

O1   -500! CORNETO M·I·279·7

O2   +890 CLONMACNOISE B·A·E·V·5

O3   +890 CLONMACNOISE B·A·E·V·5

O4   +950 CLONMACNOISE B·A·E·V·5

O5   O6   BR. TRANSCAUCASIA ON BOWL Z·E·1905 142

O7   -3500 UR

O8   -600 MT SANNACE G·BA·V·6

O9   G·C·C·I·22 CAPPADOCIA

P1   N. APULIA R·I·xLvii,250

P2   -500 CORNETO, M·I·279·7

P3   N. APULIAN. M·AP·XVII 10

P4   CAPPADOCIA G·C·C·I·74

P5   CAPPADOCIA G·C·C·II 9451

P6   CAPPADOCIA G·C·C·I·73

P8   FE.I. OEDENBURG HUNGARY D·F·218

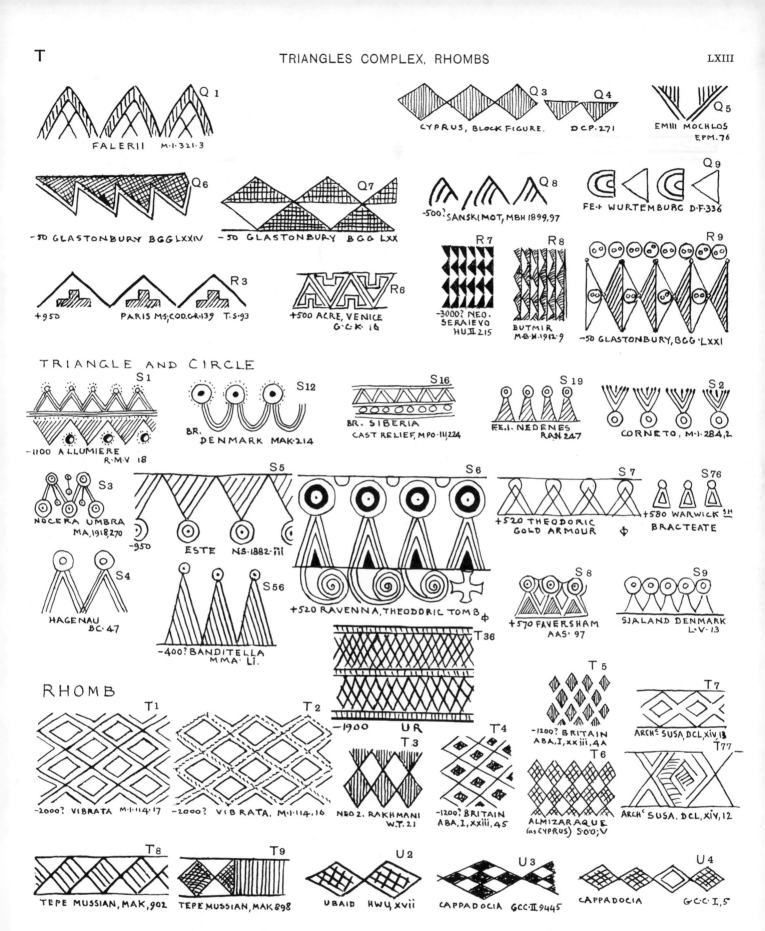

Q1 FALERII M·I·321·3

Q3 CYPRUS, BLOCK FIGURE.

Q4 DCP·271

Q5 EMIII MOCHLOS EPM·76

Q6 -50 GLASTONBURY BGG LXXIV

Q7 -50 GLASTONBURY BGG LXX

Q8 -500? SANSKI MOT, MBH 1899,97

Q9 FE-I WURTEMBURG D·F·336

R3 +950 PARIS MS; COD.GR·139 T·S·93

R6 +500 ACRE, VENICE G·C·K 16

R7 -3000? NEO. SERAIEVO HU·II 215

R8 BUTMIR M·B·H·1912·9

R9 -50 GLASTONBURY, BGG LXXI

TRIANGLE AND CIRCLE

S1 -1100 ALLUMIERE R·M·V 18

S12 BR. DENMARK MAK·214

S16 BR. SIBERIA CAST RELIEF, MPO·III/224

S19 FE·I. NEDENES RAN 247

S2 CORNETO, M·I·284,2

S3 NOCERA UMBRA MA,1918,270

S5 -950 ESTE NS·1882·711

S6 +520 RAVENNA, THEODORIC TOMB φ

S7 +520 THEODORIC GOLD ARMOUR

S76 +580 WARWICK SH BRACTEATE

S4 HAGENAU BC·47

S56 -400? BANDITELLA MMA Li.

S8 +570 FAVERSHAM AAS·97

S9 SJALAND DENMARK L·V·13

RHOMB

T36

T1 -2000? VIBRATA M·I·114·17

T2 -2000? VIBRATA, M·I·114,16

-1900 UR

T3 NEO 2. RAKHMANI W·T·21

T4 -1200? BRITAIN ABA,I,xxiii,45

T5 -1200? BRITAIN ABA,I,xxiii,4A

T6 ALMIZARAQUE (as CYPRUS) 500;V

T7 ARCH^c SUSA, DCL, XIV, 13

T77 ARCH^c SUSA, DCL, XIV, 12

T8 TEPE MUSSIAN, MAK,902

T9 TEPE MUSSIAN, MAK 898

U2 UBAID HWY XVII

U3 CAPPADOCIA GCC·II 9445

U4 CAPPADOCIA G·C·C·I,5

U5 -1200? BRITAIN ABA,I,XXIV,60

U6 -700 CRETE ABS VIII

U7 FALERII M·I·320,14

U8 -700 ATHENS K·B·116

U9 CAPUA K·T·50

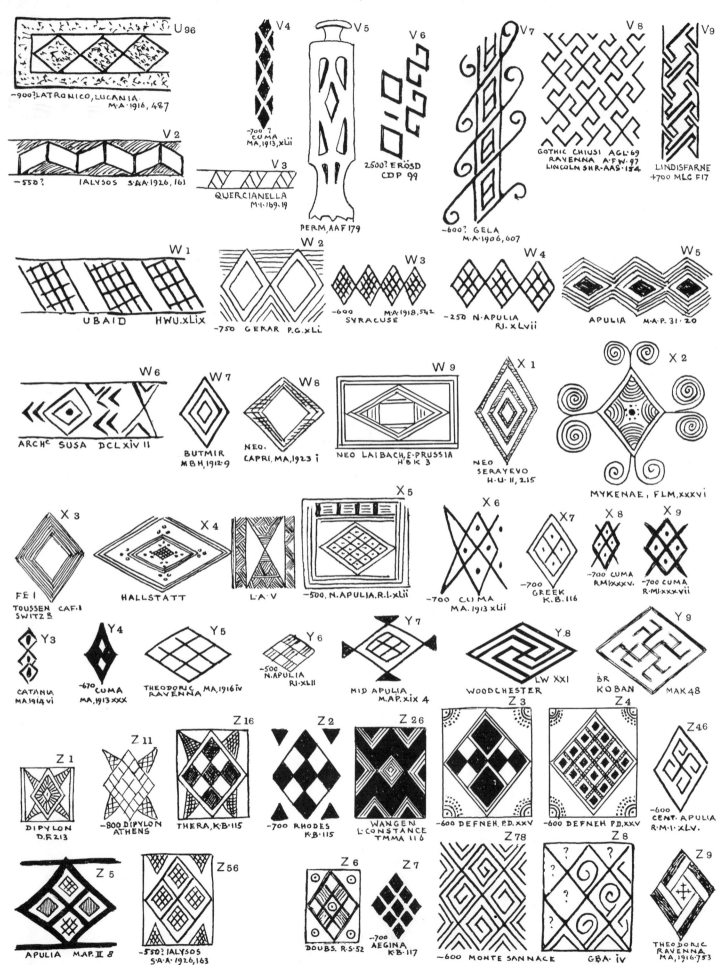

U 96 — -900? LATRONICO, LUCANIA. M·A·1916, 487

V 2 — -550? IALYSOS S·A·A·1926, 161

V 4 — -700? CUMA MA, 1913, xLii

V 3 — QUERCIANELLA M·Y·169·19

V 5 — PERM, AAF 179

V 6 — 2500? ERÖSD CDP 99

V 7 — -600? GELA M·A·1906, 607

V 8 — GOTHIC CHIUSI AGL·69 RAVENNA A·F·W·97 LINCOLN SHR·AAS·154

V 9 — LINDISFARNE +700 MLC F17

W 1 — UBAID HWU·xLix

W 2 — -750 GEKAR P·G·xLi

W 3 — -600 SYRACUSE M·A·1918, 542

W 4 — -250 N·APULIA RJ·xLvii

W 5 — APULIA M·A·P· 31·20

W 6 — ARCHᶜ SUSA DCL xiv 11

W 7 — BUTMIR MBH, 1912·9

W 8 — NEO. CAPRI, MA, 1923 i

W 9 — NEO LAIBACH, E·PRUSSIA H·B·K 3

X 1 — NEO SERAYEVO H·U· II, 2.15

X 2 — MYKENAE, FLM, xxxvi

X 3 — FE 1 TOUSSEN CAF·1 SWITZᴿ

X 4 — HALLSTATT

— L·A·V

X 5 — -500, N·APULIA·R·I·xLii

X 6 — -700 CUMA MA·1913 xLii

X 7 — -700 GREEK K·B·116

X 8 — -700 CUMA RMixxxv·

X 9 — -700 CUMA R·MI·xxxvii

Y 3 — CATANIA MA·1914 vi

Y 4 — -670 CUMA MA, 1913 xxx

Y 5 — THEODORIC MA, 1916 iv RAVENNA

Y 6 — -500 N·APULIA RJ·xLII

Y 7 — MID APULIA M·A·P· xix 4

Y 8 — WOODCHESTER LW XXI

Y 9 — BR KOBAN MAK 48

Z 1 — DIPYLON D·F· 213

Z 11 — -800 DIPYLON ATHENS

Z 16 — THERA, K·B·115

Z 2 — -700 RHODES K·B·115

Z 26 — WANGEN L·CONSTANCE TMMA 116

Z 3 — -600 DEFNEH. P·D· xxv

Z 4 — -600 DEFNEH P·D·xxv

Z 46 — -600 CENT·APULIA R·M·I· xLv.

Z 5 — APULIA M·A·P· II 8

Z 56 — -550? IALYSOS S·A·A·1926, 163

Z 6 — DOUBS. R·S·52

Z 7 — -700 AEGINA K·B·117

Z 78 — -600 MONTE SANNACE

Z 8 — GBA· iv

Z 9 — THEODORIC RAVENNA MA, 1916·753

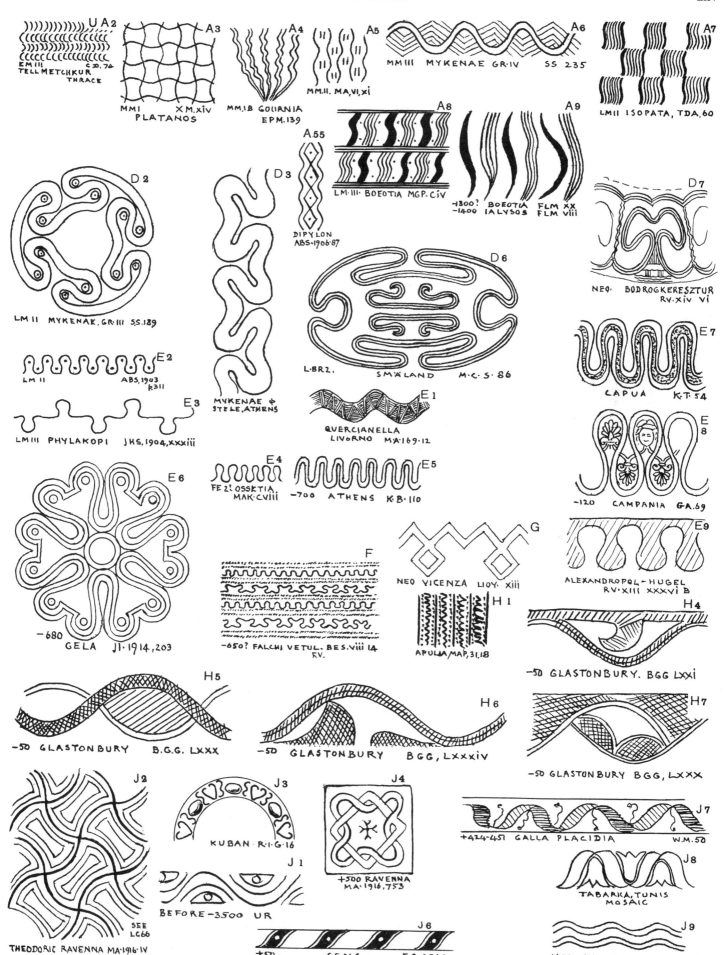

UA2
EM.III   C.XI.74
TELL METCHKUR
THRACE

A3
MM.I   XM.xiv
PLATANOS

A4
MM.IB GOURNIA
EPM.139

A5
MM.II. MA.VI.xi

A6
MM.III   MYKENAE GR.IV   SS 235

A7
LM.II ISOPATA, TDA.60

A8
LM.III. BOEOTIA MGP.CIV

A9
+1300?   BOEOTIA   FLM XX
-1400   IALYSOS   FLM viii

A.55
DIPYLON
ABS.1906.87

D2
LM.II   MYKENAE, GR.III   S.S.189

D3
MYKENAE Φ
STELE, ATHENS

D6
L.BR2.   SMÄLAND   M·C·S·86

D7
NEO.   BODROGKERESZTUR
RV·XIV VI

E2
LM II   ABS,1903
P311

E3
LM.III PHYLAKOPI   JHS,1904,xxxiii

E1
QUERCIANELLA
LIVORNO   MA.169·12

E7
CAPUA   K.T.54

E8
-120   CAMPANIA   GA.69

E6
-680   GELA   JI·1914,203

E4
FE.2? OSSETIA
MAK·CVIII

E5
-700   ATHENS   K·B·110

E9
ALEXANDROPOL–HUGEL
RV·XIII XXXVI B

G
NEO VICENZA LIOY. Xiii

F
-650? FALCHI VETUL. BES·viii 14
F.V.

H1
APULIA/MAP, 31,18

H4
-50 GLASTONBURY. BGG LXXI

H5
-50 GLASTONBURY   B.G.G. LXXX

H6
-50 GLASTONBURY   BGG, LXXXIV

H7
-50 GLASTONBURY BGG, LXXX

J2
SEE
LC66
THEODORIC RAVENNA MA·1916· IV

J3
KUBAN R·I·G·16

J1
BEFORE -3500   UR

J4
+500 RAVENNA
MA·1916,753

J6
+50   SENS   E·G·2760

J7
+424-451 GALLA PLACIDIA   W.M.50

J8
TABARKA, TUNIS
MOSAIC

J9
+600 NOCERA   MA.1918,175

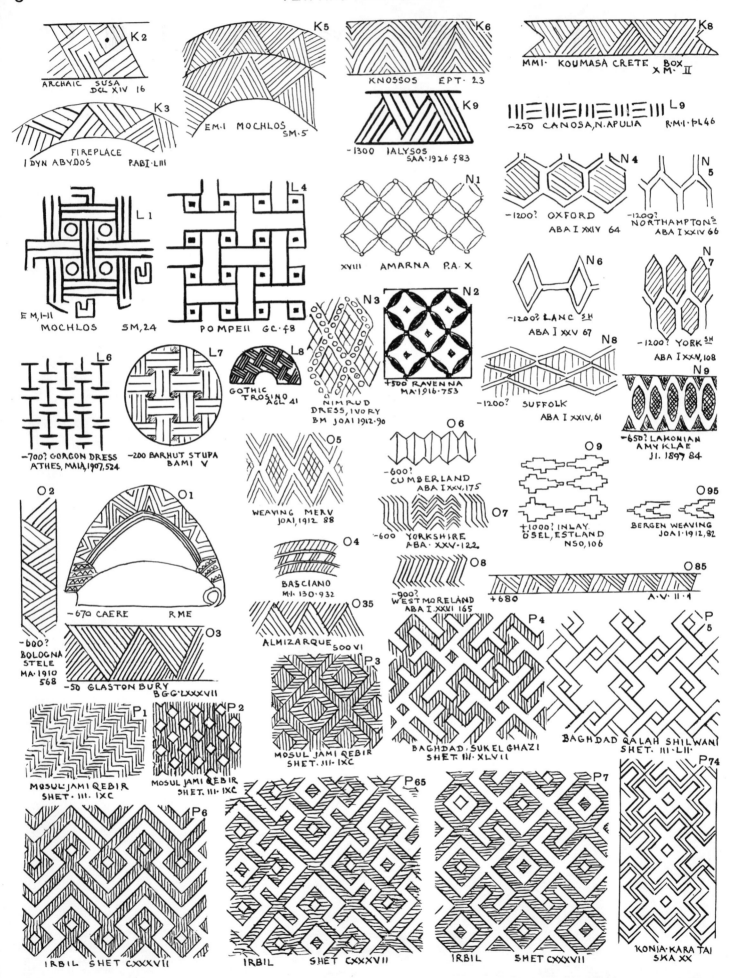

K2 ARCHAIC SUSA DCL XIV 16

K3 FIREPLACE I DYN ABYDOS P.ABI·LIII

K5 EM·I MOCHLOS SM·5

K6 KNOSSOS EPT·23

K9 -1300 IALYSOS SAA·1926 f83

K8 MMI· KOUMASA CRETE ×M·II BOX

L9 -250 CANOSA,N·APULIA R·M·I·PL46

L1 E M, I-II MOCHLOS SM,24

L4 POMPEII GC·f8

N1 XVIII AMARNA P.A·X

N4 -1200? OXFORD ABA I XXIV 64

N5 -1200? NORTHAMPTONS ABA I XXIV 66

N6 -1200? LANC SH ABA I XXV 67

N7 -1200? YORK SH ABA I XXV,108

N3 NIMRUD DRESS,IVORY BM JOAI 1912·90

N2 +500 RAVENNA MA·1916·753

N8 -1200? SUFFOLK ABA I XXIV,61

N9 -650? LAKONIAN AMYKLAE JI. 1897 84

L6 -700? GORGON DRESS ATHES, MAIA,1907,524

L7 -200 BARHUT STUPA BAMI V

L8 GOTHIC TROSINO AGL 41

O5 WEAVING MERV JOAI,1912 88

O6 -600? CUMBERLAND ABA I XXV,175

O7 -600 YORKSHIRE ABA·XXV·122·

O9 +1000? INLAY OSEL,ESTLAND NSO,106

O95 BERGEN WEAVING JOAI·1912,82

O2 -600? BOLOGNA STELE MA·1910 568

O1 -670 CAERE RME

O3 -50 GLASTONBURY BGG·LXXXVII

O4 BASCIANO M·I·130·932

O35 ALMIZARQUE 500 VI

O8 -900? WESTMORELAND ABA I XXVI 165

O85 +680 A·V·II·1

P4 BAGHDAD·SUK EL GHAZI SHET·III·XLVII

P5 BAGHDAD QALAH SHILWANI SHET·III·LII

P3 MOSUL JAMI QEBIR SHET·III·IXC

P1 MOSUL JAMI QEBIR SHET·III·IXC

P2 MOSUL JAMI QEBIR SHET·III·IXC

P6 IRBIL SHET CXXXVII

P65 IRBIL SHET CXXXVII

P7 IRBIL SHET CXXXVII

P74 KONIA·KARA TAI SKA XX

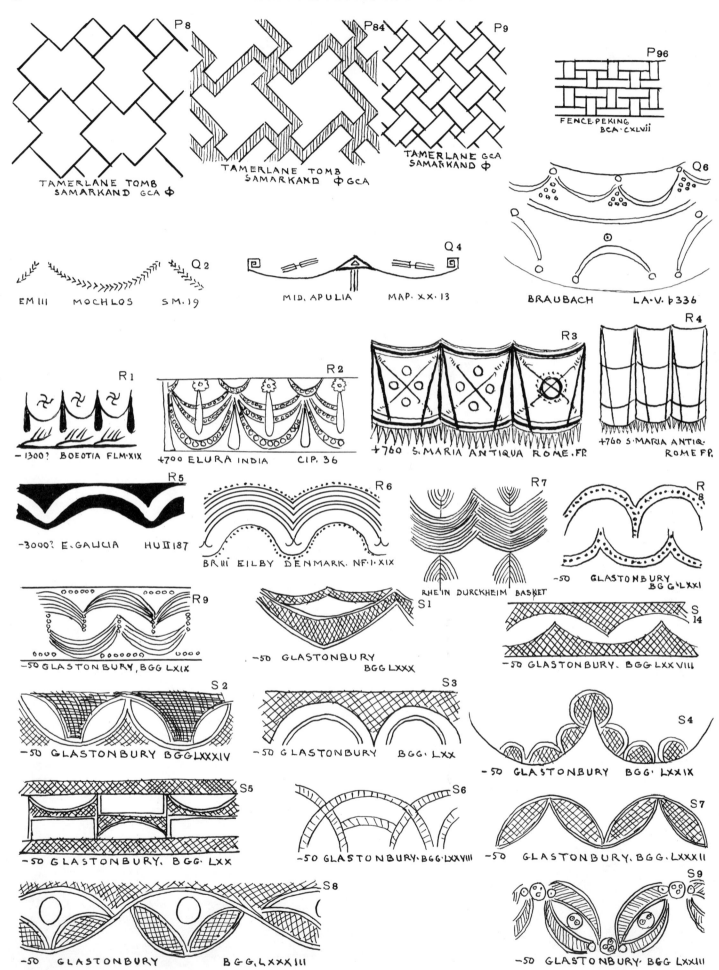

P8
TAMERLANE TOMB SAMARKAND GCA Φ

P84
TAMERLANE TOMB SAMARKAND Φ GCA

P9
TAMERLANE GCA SAMARKAND Φ

P96
FENCE PEKING BCA CXLVii

Q2
EM III   MOCHLOS   SM 19

Q4
MID APULIA   MAP XX 13

Q6
BRAUBACH   LA V b336

R1
-1300? BOEOTIA FLM XIX

R2
+700 ELURA INDIA   CIP 36

R3
+760 S MARIA ANTIQUA ROME FP

R4
+760 S MARIA ANTIQ ROME FP

R5
-3000? E GALLIA   HU II 187

R6
BR III EILBY DENMARK NF I XIX

R7
RHEIN DURCKHEIM BASKET

R8
-50 GLASTONBURY BG G LXXI

R9
-50 GLASTONBURY BGG LXIX

S1
-50 GLASTONBURY BGG LXXX

S14
-50 GLASTONBURY BGG LXXVIII

S2
-50 GLASTONBURY BGG LXXXIV

S3
-50 GLASTONBURY BGG LXX

S4
-50 GLASTONBURY BGG LXXIX

S5
-50 GLASTONBURY BGG LXX

S6
-50 GLASTONBURY BGG LXXVIII

S7
-50 GLASTONBURY BGG LXXXII

S8
-50 GLASTONBURY BGG LXXXIII

S9
-50 GLASTONBURY BGG LXXIII

T1 NEO. CAPRI MA.1923, i

T2 NEO. PATERNO CATANIA M.A.1914. vi

T3 NEO. RAKHMANI W.T.21

T4 NEO. E. GALICIA H.U.II.187

T5 NEO PATERNO CATANIA M.A.1914. III 700? ARGOS, K.B.110

T6 -1100, 200 SCV 69

T7 THEBES THESSALY W.T.113

T8 THEBES, THESSALY W.T.113

T9 700? K.B.110 MYKENAE THERA. K.B.117

U1 NEO CU. RAKHMANI W.T.13

U2 "PRIMITIVE POTTERY" AL UBAID HWUXV

U3 AS CYPRUS. ALMIZARAQUE SPAIN S.O.O. V

U4 I-II SICUL MT. TABUTO RV XIII Liv

U5 LATIUM, M.I.140.9 141.21

U7 -500 STYRIA HBK 168

U8 BRICK. TU.SAN.FU.BCA xxxvii

U27 TENE III ELCHE, D.F.2,684

V4

U6 S. APULIA M. AP. xxviii 1

U64 -450 ESTE R.M.I.5,22

U9 ARDANE C.C.O. 65

V2 NEO. LAIBACH HBK.VII

V3 NEO. GROTTA ALL'ONDA M.I.115.13

V5 LM.I. GOURNIA 3 HG. pl. I LM.I. MOCHLOS AJA 1909 282

V6 XVIII SEDMENT P5 LIX

V8 XVIII AMARNA P.A.X

W2 MMII KNOSSOS MGP. LXVIII

W3 MM.II. CRETE. MSAC III xLi Φ

W6 TARXIEN. A.1916, xix

W7 TARXIEN A.1916, xix

W8 TARXIEN A.1916 XIX

W9 TARXIEN. A.1916, xix

W4 DRESDEN MBH 1912.10 SILESIA AA.1908.IX

X7 -1300 VARDAROFTSA ABS 1926 60

X9

X2 X QAU PQ. Φ

X3 AL UBAID HWUXLIX

X4 BR. CHAUCHITSA, MACEDONIA A.1925 XXVI

X5 CAPPADOCIA G.C.C. I.31

X6 ARCHAIC SUSA DCL. XVIII 10

X8 XVIII KEFTI DRESS C.M. excl.

-600 DEFNEH P.D.XXV

Y6 CUMA M.A.1903,236

Y7 700? CRETE K.B.114

Y1 XII DAHSHUR Φ

Y2 XII HARAGEH EH XIV

Y3 -1350 VARDAROFTSA ABS 1926 60

Y4 MYKENAE ATREUS RV.VIII.CXXVI

Y5 BARBERINI M.A.1925. ii

Y54 CUMA, M.A.1903-237

Y8

Y9 +500 MIDZUO RAR 1923

-300 CHINA BRONZE VASE BMB.162

Z3 M.HELL KORAKOU B.K. iii

Z6 CAPUA K.T.35

Z7 CAPUA K.T.35

Z8 S. ANGELO. CAPUA K.T.28

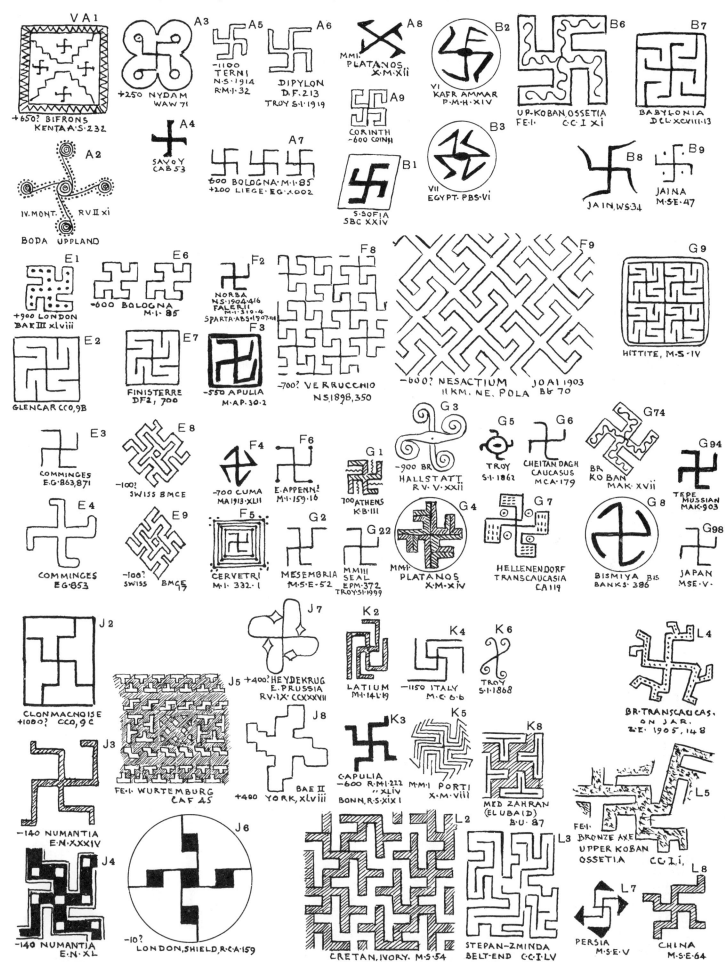

VA1 +650? BIFRONS KENTAA·S·232

A3 +250 NYDAM WAW 71

A5 –1100 TERNI N·S·1914 R·M·I·32

A6 DIPYLON D·F·213 TROY S·I·1919

A8 MMI. PLATANOS X·M·Xii

A9 CORINTH –600 COINH

B2 VI KAFR AMMAR P·M·H·XIV

B6 U·P·KOBAN OSSETIA FE·I· C·C·I·Xi

B7 BABYLONIA D·C·L·XCViii·13

A4 SAVOY CAB 53

A7 –600 BOLOGNA·M·I·85 +200 LIEGE·E·G·1002

B1 S·SOFIA SBC XXiv

B3 VII EGYPT·PBS·Vi

B8 JAIN·WS·34

B9 JAINA M·S·E·47

A2 IV. MONT. RV·II·Xi BODA UPPLAND

E1 +900 LONDON BAK III xlviii

E6 –600 BOLOGNA M·I·85

F2 NORBA N·S·1904·416 FALERII N·S·1319·4 SPARTA·ABS·1907·118

F8 –700? VERRUCCHIO N·S·1898, 350

F9 –600? NESACTIUM JO·AI 1903 11 KM. NE. POLA BG 70

G9 HITTITE, M·S·IV

E2 GLENCAR CC·0,9B

E7 FINISTERRE DF2, 700

F3 –550 APULIA M·AP·30·2

E3 COMMINGES E·G·863,871

E8 –100? SWISS BMCE

F4 –700 CUMA MA·1913·XLII

F6 E. APPENN! M·I·159·16

G1 700 ATHENS K·B·III

G3 –900 BR. HALLSTATT. RV·V·XXII

G5 TROY S·I·1862

G6 CHEITAN DAGH CAUCASUS M·C·A·179

G74 BR. KO BAN MAK·XVII

G94 TEPE MUSSIAN MAK·903

E4 COMMINGES E·G·853

E9 –100? SWISS BMCE 17

F5 CERVETRI M·I·332·1

G2 MESEMBRIA M·S·E·52

G22 MMIII SEAL EPM·372 TROY·S1·1999

G4 MMI. PLATANOS X·M·XIV

G7 HELLENENDORF TRANSCAUCASIA CA 119

G8 BISMIYA BIS BANKS·386

G98 JAPAN MSE·V·

J2 CLONMACNOISE +1000? CC·0,9 C

J7 J5 +400? HEYDEKRUG E. PRUSSIA RV·IX·CCXXXVII

K2 LATIUM M·I·141·19

K4 –1150 ITALY M·C·6·6

K6 TROY S·I·1868

L4 BR·TRANSCAUCAS. ON JAR. Z·E·1905,148

J3 –140 NUMANTIA E·N·XXXIV

J8 +400 YORK, XLViii

K3 C·APULIA –600 R·M·I·222 " xliv BONN, R·S·XiX I

K5 MMI PORTI X·M·Viii

K8 MED ZAHRAN (EL UBAID) B·U· 87

L3 FE·I· BRONZE AXE UPPER KOBAN OSSETIA CC·I,i.

L5

J4 –140 NUMANTIA E·N·XL

J6 –10? LONDON, SHIELD, R·C·A·159

L2 CRETAN, IVORY. M·S·54

STEPAN-ZMINDA BELT-END CC·I·LV

L7 PERSIA M·S·E·V

L8 CHINA M·S·E·64

FE·I· WURTEMBURG CAF 45

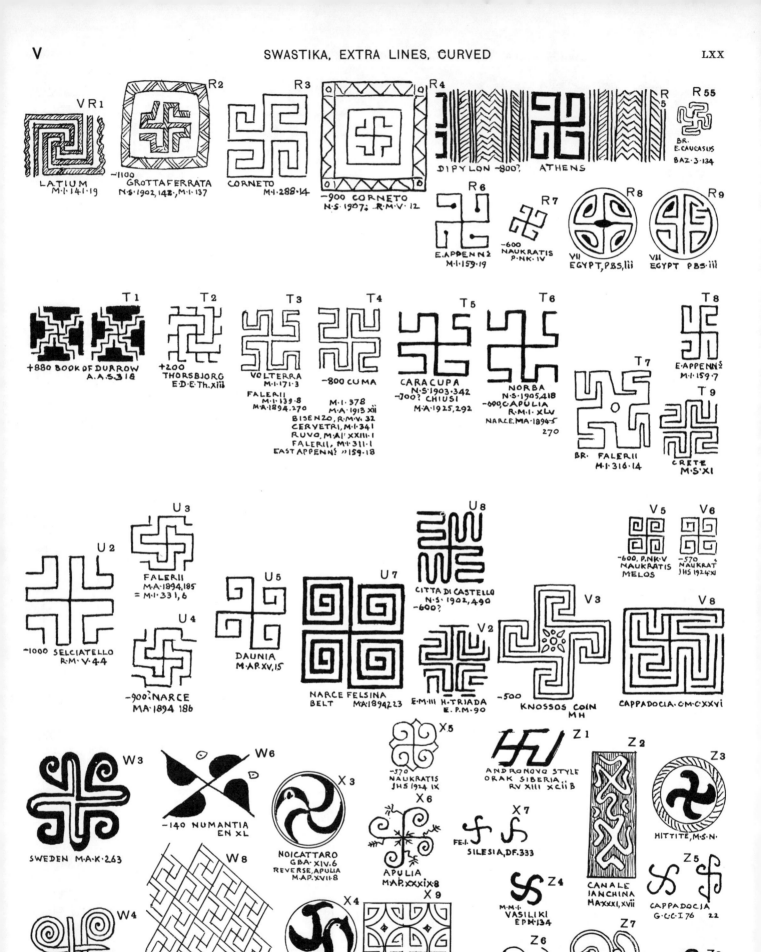

VR1 LATIUM M·I·141·19

R2 ~1100 GROTTAFERRATA N·S·1902,142; M·I·137

R3 CORNETO M·I·288·14

R4 ~900 CORNETO N·S·1907; R·M·V·12

DIPYLON ~800? ATHENS

R5

R55 BR. E.CAUCASUS BAZ·3·134

R6 E.APPENNS M·I·159·19

R7 ~600 NAUKRATIS P·NK·IV

R8 VII EGYPT, P.BS,lii

R9 VII EGYPT P.BS·iii

T1 +880 BOOK OF DURROW A.A.S·318

T2 +200 THORSBJORG E·D·E·Th·xiii

T3 VOLTERRA M·I·171·3 FALERII M·I·139·8 M·A·1894.270 BISENZO, R·M·V·32 CERVETRI, M·I·341 RUVO, M·AI·XXIII·1 FALERII, M·I·311·1 EAST APPENNS 》159·18

T4 ~800 CUMA M·I·378 M·A·1913·XII

T5 CARACUPA N·S·1903·342 ~700? CHIUSI M·A·1925,292

T6 NORBA N·S·1905,418 ~600,CAPULIA R·M·I·XLV NARCE.MA·1894·5 270

T7 BR. FALERII M·I·316·14

T8 E·APPENNS M·I·159·7

T9 CRETE M·S·XI

U2 ~1000 SELCIATELLO R·M·V·4·4

U3 FALERII M·A·1894,185 = M·I·331,6

U4 ~900? NARCE MA·1894 186

U5 DAUNIA M·AP·XV,15

U7 NARCE FELSINA BELT M·A·1894·223

U8 CITTA DI CASTELLO N·S· 1902,490 ~600?

V2 E·M·III H·TRIADA E· P·M·90

V3 ~500 KNOSSOS COIN MH

V5 ~600, P.NK·V NAUKRATIS MELOS

V6 ~570 NAUKRAT JHS 1924·XI

V8 CAPPADOCIA·CM·C·XXVI

W3 SWEDEN M·A·K·263

W6 ~140 NUMANTIA EN XL

W8 TENEI MARNE HELMET, DF2 490

W4 +1100 CONCHAN MANX CROSS X·62

X3 NOICATTARO GBA·XIV·6 REVERSE, APULIA M·AP·XVII·8

X4 ~600 M! SANNACE GBA· III·6 PEUKETIA M·AP· XXIV,3a

X5 ~570 NAUKRATIS JHS 1924·IX

X6 APULIA M·AP·XXXIX·8

X7 FE·I. SILESIA,DF·333

X9 +500 RAVENNA MA· 1916·753

Z1 ANDRONOVO STYLE ORAK SIBERIA RV XIII XCIIB

Z2 CANALE IANCHINA MA·XXXI,xvii

Z3 HITTITE, M·S·N·

Z4 M·M·I VASILIKI E·P·M·134

Z5 CAPPADOCIA G·C·C·I 76 22

Z6 CRETE E·P·M·II·107

Z7 CRETE E·P·M·II, 107

Z8 LEH. M·S·E·vi

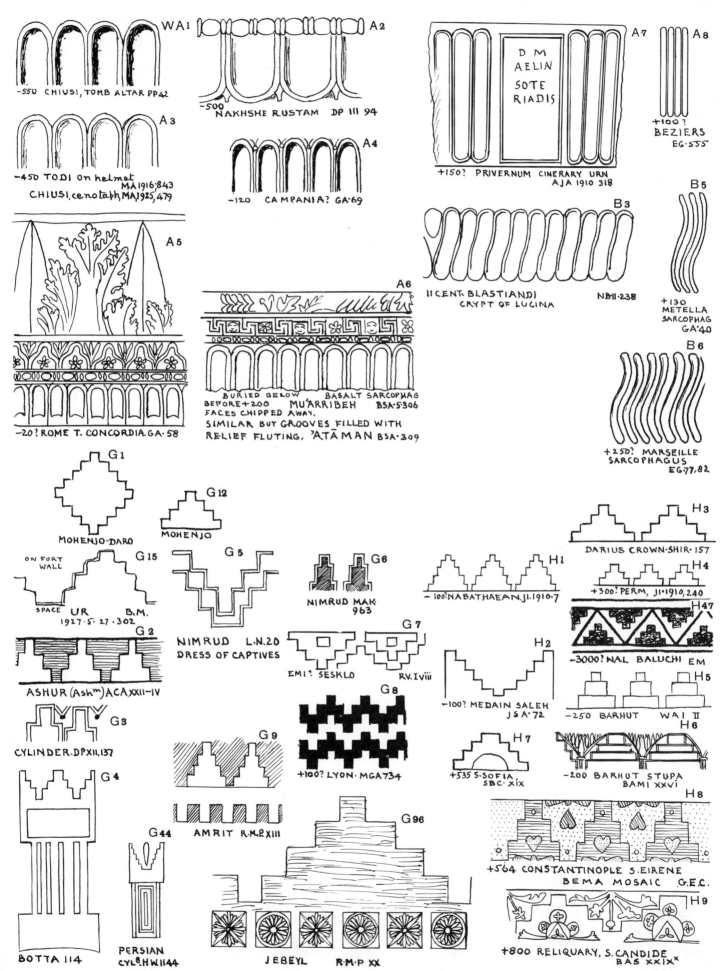

WA1 −550 CHIUSI, TOMB ALTAR PP.42

A2 −500 NAKHSHE RUSTAM DP III 94

A3 −450 TODI on helmet MA 1916.843
CHIUSI, cenotaph, MA 1925,479

A4 −120 CAMPANIA? GA.69

A7 +150? PRIVERNUM CINERARY URN
AJA 1910 318
D M AELIN SOTE RIADIS

A8 +100?
BEZIERS
EG.555

A5

A6 BURIED BELOW BASALT SARCOPHAG.
BEFORE +200 MU'ARRIBEH BSA.5.306
FACES CHIPPED AWAY.
SIMILAR BUT GROOVES FILLED WITH
RELIEF FLUTING, 'ATĀMAN BSA.309

−20? ROME T. CONCORDIA. GA.58

B3 II CENT. BLASTIANDI NB II.238
CRYPT OF LUCINA

B5 +130 METELLA
SARCOPHAG.
GA.40

B6 +250? MARSEILLE
SARCOPHAGUS
EG 77,82

G1 MOHENJO-DARO

G12 MOHENJO

G15 ON FORT WALL SPACE UR B.M.
1927.5.27.302

G2 ASHUR (Ashᵐ) ACA XXII−IV

G3 CYLINDER. DP XII,137

G4 BOTTA 114

G44 PERSIAN
CYLᴿ H W II 144

G5 NIMRUD L.N.20
DRESS OF CAPTIVES

G6 NIMRUD MAK.
963

G7 EM I? SESKLO RV. I viii

G8 +100? LYON. MGA 734

G9 AMRIT R.M.P. XIII

G96 JEBEYL R.M.P XX

H1 −100? NABATHAEAN. JI.1910.7

H2 −100? MEDAIN SALEH
JSA.72

H7 +535 S.SOFIA
SBC.xix

H3 DARIUS CROWN.SHIR.157

H4 +300? PERM, JI.1910,240

H47 −3000? NAL BALUCHI EM

H5 −250 BARHUT WAI II

H6 −200 BARHUT STUPA
BAMI XXVI

H8 +564 CONSTANTINOPLE S.EIRENE
BEMA MOSAIC G.E.C.

H9 +800 RELIQUARY, S.CANDIDE
BAS XXIXˣ

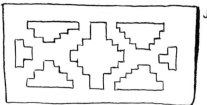

J1

+600 HEJNUM GOTLAND
OPEN WORK NSO 40

J3

LOT ET GARONNE. AFW
coarse SARAGOSSA 82

J4

W. SWITZERLAND
GARNET. AFW·102

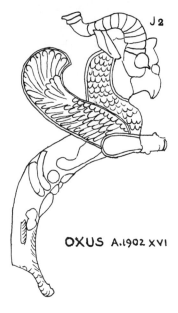

J2

OXUS A.1902 XVI

J5

GOTHIC. ITALY. AGL. 13
GARNET IN GOLD

J7

BR. MARIASSOVA
MM XXX

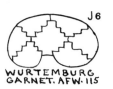

J6

WURTEMBURG
GARNET. AFW. 115

J9

LOMBARD BELLUNO
GARNET AGL 128

J8

CAUCASUS AFW.3
GARNET BOSS

J83

+480 CHILDERIC
AFW 62
CAC. p.104

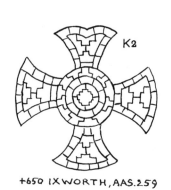

K2

+650 IXWORTH, AAS.259

K4

+700   MLG 211
LINDIS FARNF

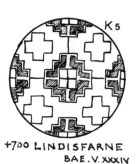

K5

+700 LINDISFARNE
BAE. V. XXXIV

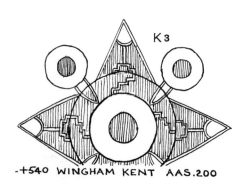

K3

-+540 WINGHAM KENT AAS.200

K7

TIBETAN W. OF PEKIN   BCA·14   L
4 STEP HONAN· BCAXL· 6 STEP SZECHUAN

K8

MODERN CHINA
YEN-CHOU-FU
BCA xxxiii

K9

FRANKFORT TOWN-HALL ⊕

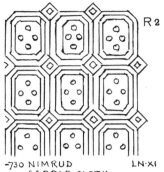

R2

-730 NIMRUD
SADDLE CLOTH   LN·XI

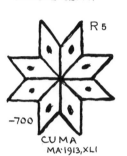

R5

-700
CUMA
MA·1913,XLI

R6

+500?RIFEH
PGR,XXXVII 8

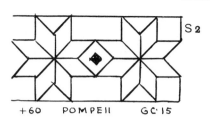

R8

SARDINIA, ALGHERO
NS·1904·333

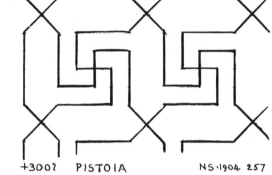

S3

+60? POMPEII   GC·14

S4

+300? PISTOIA   NS·1904 257

S2

+60   POMPEII   GC·15

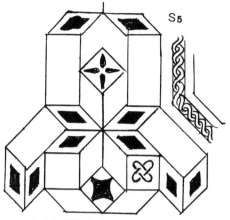

S5

ROME, VIA TUSCOLANA.   NS·1905·72

S8

+340 ROME, S.COSTANZA   Φ

T1

+400
RAVENNA
HONORIUS   MA·1916·766

T2

+500 RAVENNA   MA·1916,759
THEODORIC

S9

+100? NENNIG   GM.20

T3

+500 RAVENNA
THEODORIC   MA·1916·758

T5

+500 RAVENNA   MA·1916,751
THEODORIC

T6

+500 RAVENNA
THEODORIC MA·1916·790

T7

+800 GOSPEL OF
CHARLEMAGNE
AJA 1920 152

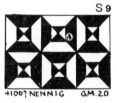

T8

+820 SOISSONS GOSPEL
AJA 1920 152

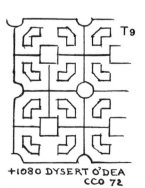

T9

+1080 DYSERT O'DEA
CCO 72

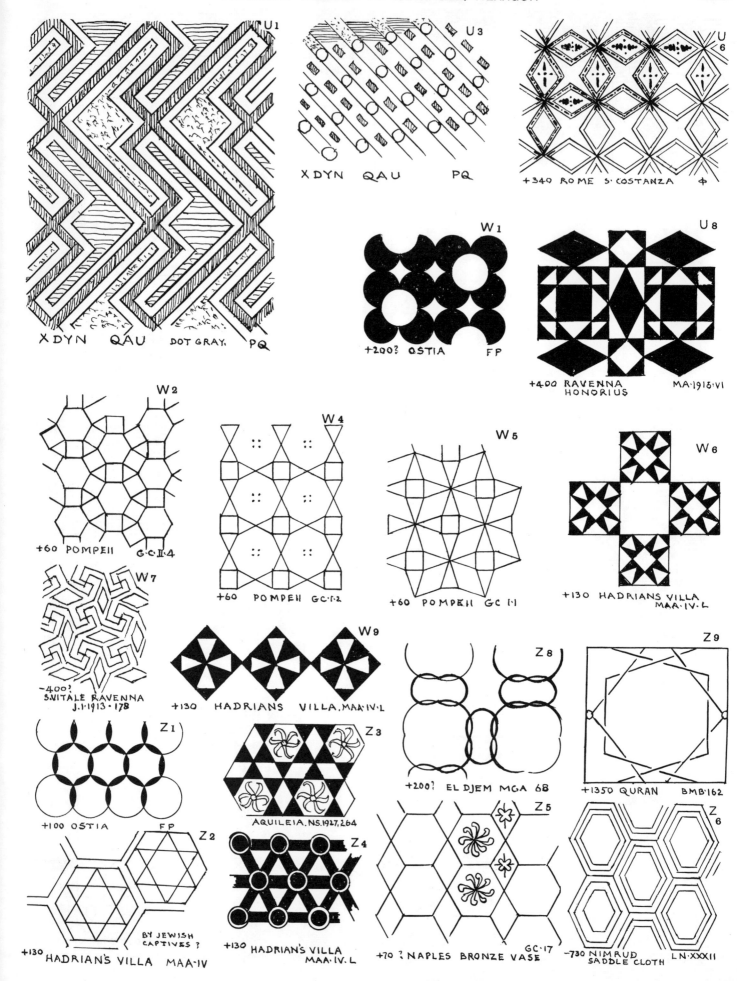

U1   X DYN QAU   DOT GRAY.   PQ

U3   X DYN QAU   PQ

U6   +340 ROME S·COSTANZA   Φ

W1   +200? OSTIA   FP

U8   +400 RAVENNA HONORIUS   MA·1915·VI

W2   +60 POMPEII   G·C·II·4

W4   +60 POMPEII GC·I·2

W5   +60 POMPEII GC I·I

W6   +130 HADRIANS VILLA MAA·IV·L

W7   −400? S·VITALE RAVENNA J·I·1913·178

W9   +130 HADRIANS VILLA, MAA·IV·L

Z8   +200? EL DJEM MGA 68

Z9   +1350 QURAN   BMB·162

Z1   +100 OSTIA   FP

Z3   AQUILEIA. NS.1927,264

Z2   +130 HADRIAN'S VILLA MAA·IV

Z4   +130 HADRIAN'S VILLA MAA·IV·L

Z5   +70? NAPLES BRONZE VASE   GC·17

Z6   −730 NIMRUD SADDLE CLOTH   LN·XXXII

BY JEWISH CAPTIVES ?

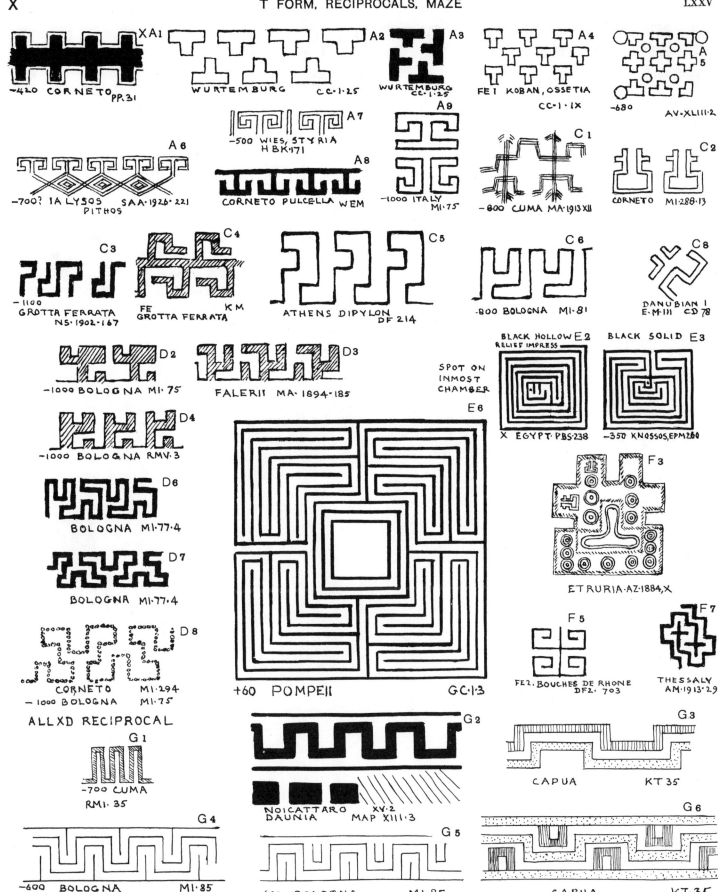

-420 CORNETO PP.31 XA1

WURTEMBURG   CC·1·25 A2

WURTEMBURG CC·1·25 A3

FE1 KOBAN, OSSETIA A4 CC·1·IX

-680 A5 AV·XLIII·2

-500 WIES, STYRIA A7 HBK·171

-700? IALYSOS PITHOS SAA·1926·221 A6

CORNETO PULCELLA WEM A8

-1000 ITALY MI·75 A9

-800 CUMA MA·1913·XII C1

CORNETO MI·288·13 C2

-1100 GROTTA FERRATA NS·1902·167 C3

FE GROTTA FERRATA KM C4

ATHENS DIPYLON DF·214 C5

-800 BOLOGNA MI·81 C6

DANUBIAN I E·M·III CD·78 C8

-1000 BOLOGNA MI·75 D2

FALERII MA·1894·185 D3

SPOT ON INMOST CHAMBER E6

BLACK HOLLOW E2 RELIEF IMPRESS

BLACK SOLID E3

X EGYPT PBS·238

-350 KNOSSOS EPM·260

-1000 BOLOGNA RMV·3 D4

BOLOGNA MI·77·4 D6

BOLOGNA MI·77·4 D7

ETRURIA AZ·1884·X F3

CORNETO MI·294 -1000 BOLOGNA MI·75 D8

+60 POMPEII GC·1·3 E6

FE5 F5

FE2·BOUCHES DE RHONE DF2·703

THESSALY AM·1913·29 F7

ALL XD RECIPROCAL

-700 CUMA RMI·35 G1

NOICATTARO XV·2 DAUNIA MAP XIII·3 G2

CAPUA KT·35 G3

-600 BOLOGNA MI·85 G4

-600 BOLOGNA MI·85 G5

CAPUA KT·35 G6

-680 CENTRAL APULIA GBA·II·1 -600 MONTE SANNACE G7

KAMEIROS ABS·1906·72 G8

APULIA MAP·I·2 DAUNIA MAP·XII·14 G9

XK2   +440 RAVENNA PLACIDIA Φ

K5   FE·I· NANCY   DF 219   HAUTE MARNE DF 247

K7   SEE LX8   CLONMACNOISE CCO 7B

L2   −600 S·APULIA RM1·45

L3   −500 ESTE BRONZE STUDS R·M1·4·5

L4   LATIUM M·1·140·9 DAUNIA MAP XIII·4 VOLTERRA, MI·171·1

L5   CAPUA KT·40

L6   −2000? VIBRATA M·I· 114,18

L7   −700? ATHENS   K·B·110 MA·1913·XXXIX / −700? CUMA / −500 CAULONIA MA·1923·471

L8   −800 BOLOGNA RMV·7

L9   −600 BOLOGNA M1·85

M7   −600 ESTE MA 1887·137

M2   BR. BODROGKERESZTUR ON GODROONED BOWL   RV II TOKAY

M3   FEZ. FINISTERRE DF2·700

M6   XDYN   QAU   PQ

M8   XDYN   QAU   PQ

M4   CLONMACNOISE CCO·7A

M5   −600 BOLOGNA M1·85   RAVENNA, S·APOL·N· MAP XXVII

N3   CAPUA KT·33

N5   CAPUA KT54

O3   VALENZANO GBA·XII·5

O6   MID APULIA MAP. XIX O

O7

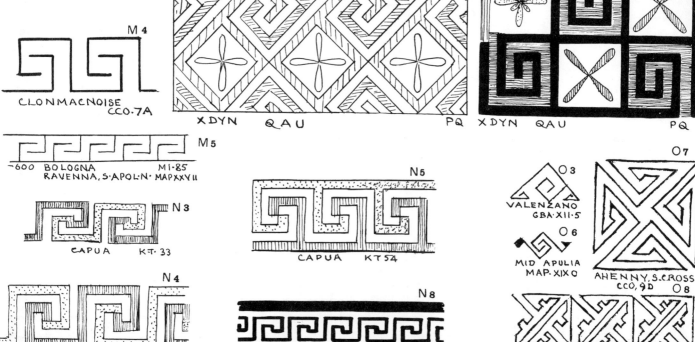

N4   −700 CRETE   CAPUA KT40 ABS VIII

N8   +520 RAVENNA S·APOL·NUOV· Φ

AHENNY, S.CROSS CCO.9D   O8

+924 MONASTERBOICE MUIRDACH CCO 7G

CERVETRI MI·340·4   XP2

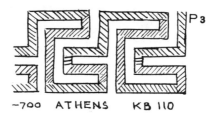

−700 ATHENS   KB 110   P3

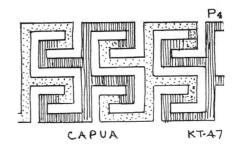

CAPUA   KT·47   P4

−700? ATHENS AZ·1884·IX   P6

HALLSTATT   BC 57   P7

HALLSTATT, SCABBARD BC·57   P8

−600   ESTE BRONZE STUDS. MA 1897.139.   P9

RHODES. KB 114   T1

−600? KARIA, HU II, 246   T2

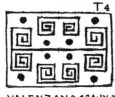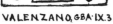

CROPTHORNE CROSS HEAD BEQ 38   +800?   T3

VALENZANO, GBA·IX.3   T4

CAMBRIDGE A·1925,245   T5

−670 CAERE ROME   T6

+1080 CCO.56 DYSERT O'DEA DIAGONAL AT FERNS   T7

MEIGLE   RCA 286   T8

CARDONAGH, CCO.51   T9

−500 ATHENS DRESS   Φ   U2

N·CHINA SCREEN. BCA ALSO RHOMBIC CLXIII   U4

+100? AIX PROVENCE MGA·47   U5

MM III KNOSSOS   EPM.256   U6

−450 SYRACUSE   U3

+440 RAVENNA, PLACIDIA   Φ   U7

+440 RAVENNA, PLACIDIA NB·II·152   U8

+101 IS-SANAMEN   BSA·5·XIX   U9

XV 3

CAPUA   KT 53

V 4

CAPUA   KT 40

V 6

CAPUA   KT·55

V 7

+200 INKHIL
+60 POMPEII

BSA·5·286,314
GC·II·3

V 8

+500? RIFEH   PGR·XXXVII B

W 1

BAWYT   GcClII

W 2

-700 RHODES   K·B·115

W 3

+200 OXYRHYNKHOS COLONNADE

W 4

PTC·
XXXV

W 6

-300 CALTAGIRONE   MA·1922·117

W 7

-500 LANUVIUM
MA 1921·322

W 8

-600 NAUKRATIS   PNK·IV
POLEMARKHOS

W 9

-570 DAFNEH   PD·XXXII

X 3

-500 CAULONIA MA·1923,440

X 5

VULCI   DA 188
C·METELLA   GA 60
CAPUA   KT 53

X 6

+40?   VASE   GA 49

X 7

-500 CAULONIA   MA 1923·442
+500 OXYRHYNKHOS PTCXLVII

X 8

CAPUA   KT·53

Y 3

Y 5

XII DYN SIUT   MS·71

Y 8

ESTE II NESACTIUM ISTRIA
RV·VIII d

JDE·38

Z 1

-600   MONTE SANNACE GBA XLIV

Z 2

-600   MONTE SANNACE, GBA XLIV

Z 3

Z 4

-600? PRAESOS
ABS·1906·50

Z 5

-600
Mt SANNACE
GBA·V·3

Z 6

SIEBENBÜRGEN   ZE 1907·115

AEGINA
AZ·1882 IX

Z 56

NEO MEZINE
RV·XIII, XVI   -50 GLASTONBURY
BGG LXXXVI

Z 7

Y 6

-650   KOBAN UPPER OSSETIA   CC·I·XX"

Z 8

MÄHREN   MBH,1912,59

Z 9

BULGARIA   MS·85

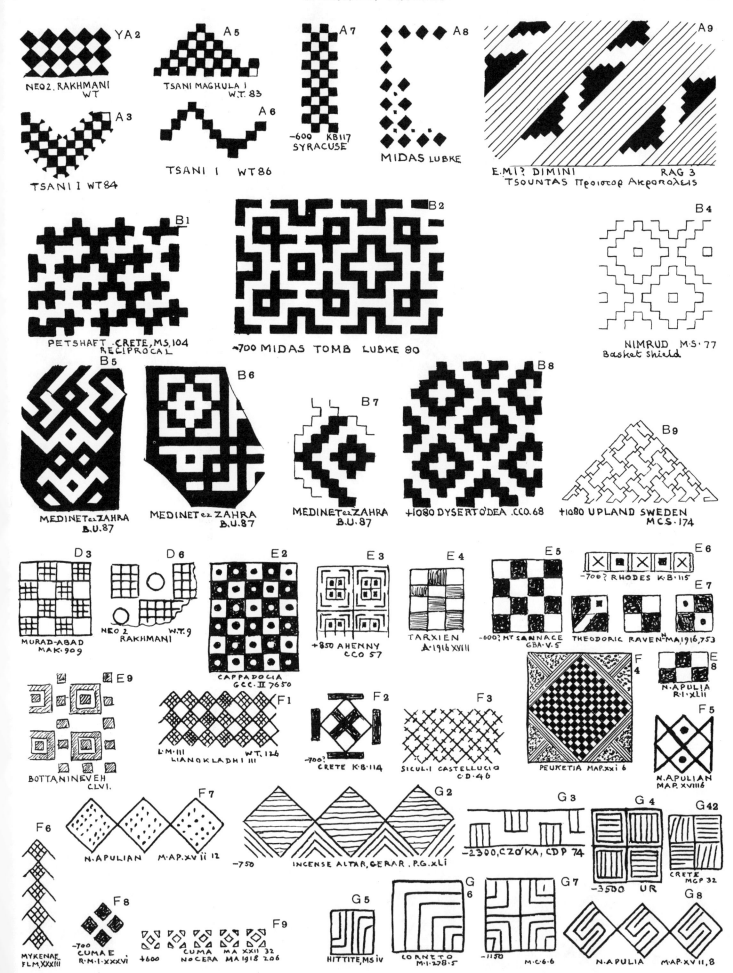

YA2 NEO2. RAKHMANI WT

A3 TSANI I WT84

A5 TSANI MAGHULA I W.T. 83

A6 TSANI I WT86

A7 -600 KB117 SYRACUSE

A8 MIDAS LUBKE

A9 E.MI? DIMINI TSOUNTAS Προιστορ Ακροπολεις RAG 3

B1 PETSHAFT CRETE, MS, 104 RECIPROCAL

B2 -700 MIDAS TOMB LUBKE 90

B4 NIMRUD M·S·77 Basket shield

B5 MEDINET ez ZAHRA B.U.87

B6 MEDINET ez ZAHRA B.U.87

B7 MEDINET ez ZAHRA B.U.87

B8 +1080 DYSERTO'DEA .CCO.68

B9 +1080 UPLAND SWEDEN MCS.174

D3 MURAD-ABAD MAK.909

D6 NEO 2 RAKHMANI W.T.9

E2 CAPPADOCIA GCC.II 7650

E3 +850 AHENNY CCO 57

E4 TARXIEN A·1916 XVIII

E5 -600? MT SANNACE GBA·V·5

E6 -700? RHODES K.B·115

E7 THEODORIC RAVEN-MA1916,753

E9 BOTTA,NINEVEH CLVI.

F1 L·M·III LIANOKLADHI III W.T.126

F2 -700? CRETE K·B·114

F3 SICULI CASTELLUCIO C·D·46

F4 PEUKETIA MAP.xxi 6

E8 N.APULIA R·I·XLII

F5 N.APULIAN MAP. XVIII6

F6 MYKENAE FLM.XXXIII

F7 N.APULIAN M.AP.xVii 12

F8 -700 CUMAE R·M·I·XXXVi

F9 +600 CUMA NOCERA MA XXII 32 MA 1918 206

G2 -750 INCENSE ALTAR,GERAR .P.G.xLi

G3 -2300,CZO'KA, CDP 74

G4 -3500 UR

G42 CRETE MGP 32

G5 HITTITE,MS iv

G6 CORNETO M·I·278·5

G7 -1150 M·C·6·6

G8 N.APULIA M.AP.XVII,8

YH2
I dyn ARMLET, P.R.T. II Vi

H3
NEOL.
PATERNO CATANIA
M·A· 1914 V

H4
−1400 IALYSOS FLM. iii

H5
−700 RHODES
K·B· 115

H7
−700? CRETE K·B·114

H6
−500 N. APULIA   R·I· xLiii

H8
N. APULIA, R·I· xLiii

J2
−2300 CZOKA, CDP 74

J6
LATIUM
M·I·141·16

J4
NORBA
M·A· 1905, 14B

J7
−600
SYRACUSE
M·A· 1918, 490

L.2
N. APULIAN
MA P. XVII 10

L3
+850 A HENNY, CCO, 69

L
−600? MT SANNACE
GBA. vi. 6

L6
−600? MT. SANNACE
GBA V

L8
ANT. R.

L9
ANT. R.

M2
MMI. PLATANOS
XM. xiii

M3
MM.I.
PLATANOS
X. M. xiv

M5
HITTITE H.H. 212

M7
−1400? IALYSOS
GLASS, SAA 1926, 93

M8
−700? KOPENHAGEN
K·B·112

M9
−700? CYPRUS
K·B·114

N 2
−570
NAUKRATIS
JHS 1924 XI

N4
−800 CHIUSI
MA·1925, 434

N5
THEODORIC RAVENN
MA 1918 753

N7
+700 HARTLEPOOL
BAE V, vi

N8
+800   CCO p. 19
CLONMACNOISE

O1
TEPE MUSSIAN
MAK, 897

O11
MOHENJO−DARO

O13
FALERII   M·I· 322·J

O2
FE
BISENZIO
KM

O24
YORUBA
ESA· V

O27
CORNETO
M·A· 1905, 678
L50

O3
NORBA
N.S. 1904, 416

O4
NORBA
N.S. 1904, 416

O5
NIMES
EG 6827

O6
−600? KARIA
HU II 246

O7
CRETE, M·S·X

O8
FE BISENZIO
KM

O9
−900 BISENZIO
M·I· 257

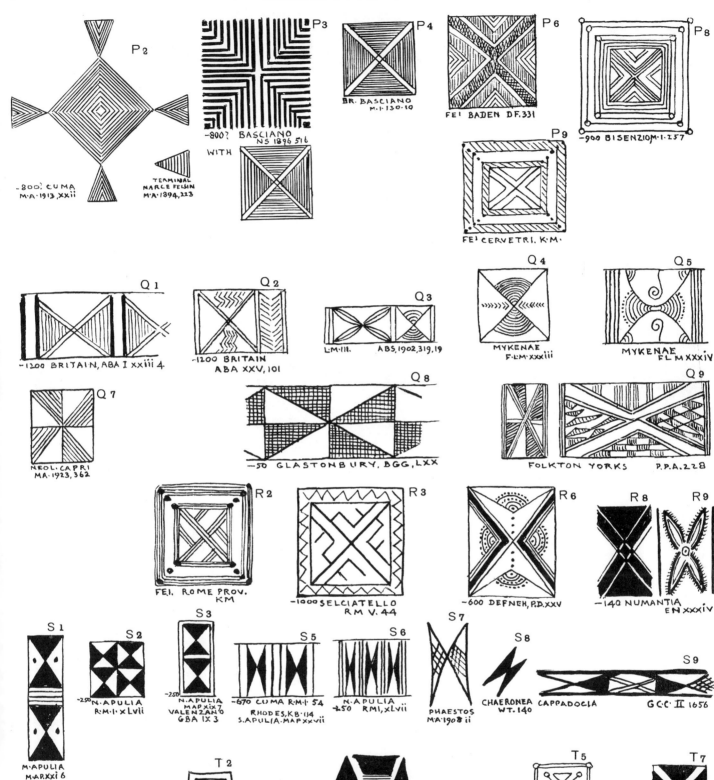

P 2

-800? CUMA
M·A·1913·XXII

TERMINAL
NARCE FELSIN
M·A·1894·223

-800? BASCIANO
NS·1896·516

WITH

P 3

P 4
BR·BASCIANO
M·I·130·10

P 6
FE¹ BADEN·D.F.331

P 8
-900 BISENZIO·M·I·257

P 9
FE¹ CERVETRI·K·M·

Q 1
-1200 BRITAIN, ABA·I·XXIII·4

Q 2
-1200 BRITAIN
ABA·XXV·101

Q 3
L·M·III.   A.B.S·1902·319·19

Q 4
MYKENAE
F·L·M·XXXIII

Q 5
MYKENAE
F·L·M·XXXIV

Q 7
NEOL·CAPRI
M·A·1923·362

Q 8
-50 GLASTONBURY, B.G.G·LXX

Q 9
FOLKTON·YORKS   P·P·A·228

R 2
FE¹·ROME·PROV·
K·M·

R 3
-1000 SELCIATELLO
R·M·V·44

R 6
~600 DEFNEH·P.D·XXV

R 8
-140 NUMANTIA
E·N·XXXIV

R 9

S 1
M·APULIA
M·A·R·XXI·6

S 2
-250 N·APULIA
R·M·I·XLVII

S 3
-250 N·APULIA
MAP·XIX·7
VALENZANO
G·B·A·IX·3

S 5
-670 CUMA·R·M·I·54
RHODES·K·B·114
S·APULIA·MAP·XXVII

S 6
N·APULIA
-250 R·M·I·XLVII

S 7
PHAESTOS
M·A·1908·II

S 8
CHAERONEA
W·T·140

CAPPADOCIA

S 9
G·C·C·II·1656

T 1
N·APULIAN
M·AP·XVIII·11

T 2
MYKENAE
F·L·M·XXVIII

T 3

ARCH⁵·SUSA·DCLXVI·11

T 4
-780 CUMA·MA·1913·XXXI

T 5
CORNETO
M·I·283·6

T 6
-140 NUMANTIA
E·N·XXXIV

T 7
TEPE·MUSSIAN
M·A·K·899
IV MILL⁰·SUSA

T 9
DAUNIA
M·A·P·XV·17

YU2   APULIA   M·AR·xLii.6

U3   PEUKETIA   M·AR·xxi 4A

U4   VALENZANO   G·BA·Xi·6

U5   -140 NUMANTIA   EN XXXVI

U6   -140 NUMANTIA   EN XXXVI

U7   S·APULIA, M·AR·xxviii.1

U8   -140 NUMANTIA   EN XXXii

V2   X DYN   QAU   PQ

V6   SEE 509   NEUMAGEN, EG·5158

V7   CAPUA   KT 55

W2   -600? KARIA   HU II 246

W3   GOTHIC PESARO   A·G·L· 3

W5   FRANKISH, SOMME   A·F·W·73

W7   LINDISFARNE   A·1925, Liii

W9   -206+25 SAC. I.   CHINA

X1   FE I CÔTE D'OR   DF 357

X3   FE I·DOUBS. DF356

X4   BR HOLSTEIN   RV·V·CV

X5   HAGENAU   BC49

X6   HAGENAU   BC·49

X7   COMMINGES   EG·890

X8   COMMINGES   EG 883

Y1   Y14   Y2   Y26   Y3   COURVEISSIAT (AIN) CAF. xxiv, BC· 54   FE·I·

Y34   HAGENAU

Y4   Y5   BC·49

Y57   HAGENAU   BC40-50

Y6   HAGENAU

Y7   BC40-50

Y8   Y9   Y95   HAGENAU   BC·40-50

Z1   Z13   Z17   HAGENAU

Z2   Z23   Z28   Z3   Z43   Z33   Z37   Z4   FE·I·   HAGENAU RHINE   BC· 48

Z5   Z54   Z6   Z64   Z7   HAGENAU   BC 40-50

Z73   Z75   HAGENAU, BC·

Z8   FE I BADEN   DF 331

Z9   -570 NAUKRATIS   JHS·1924·XI

Z93   -570 NAUKRAT   JHS·1924·XI

Z

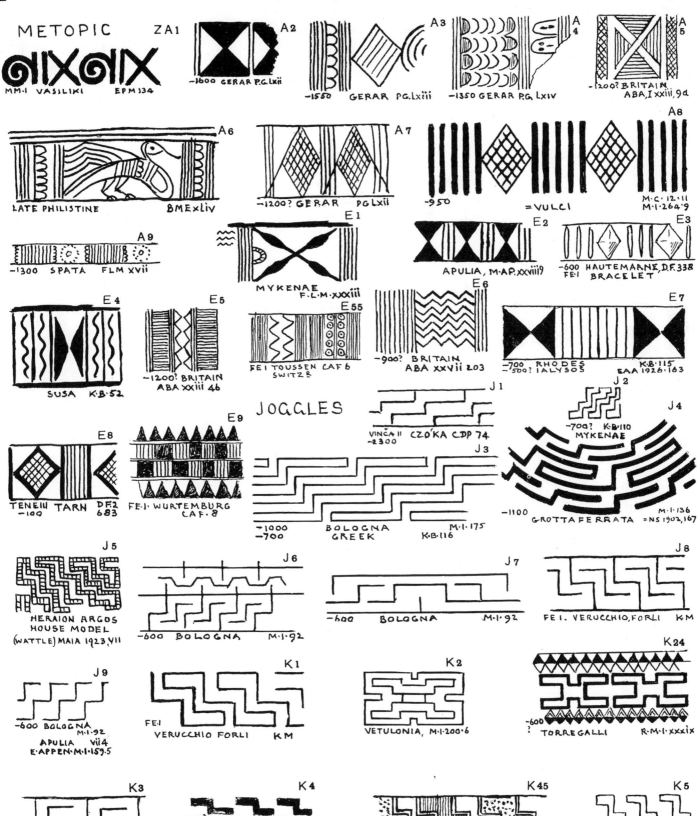

METOPIC ZA1

MM·I VASILIKI EPM 134

A2 -1600 GERAR P.G.lxii

A3 -1550 GERAR P.G.lxiii

A4 -1350 GERAR P.G. Lxiv

A5 -1200? BRITAIN ABA,I xxiii,9d

A6 LATE PHILISTINE BMExliv

A7 -1200? GERAR P.G.lxii

A8 -950 =VULCI M·C·12·11 M·I·264·9

A9 -1300 SPATA FLM XVII

E1 MYKENAE F.L.M.xxxiii

E2 APULIA, M·A·P·xxviii9

E3 -600 HAUTEMARNE, D.F.338 FE·I BRACELET

E4 SUSA K·B·52

E5 -1200? BRITAIN ABA XXIII 46

E55 FE·I TOUSSEN CAF6 SWITZ R

E6 -900? BRITAIN ABA xxvii 203

E7 -700 RHODES -500? IALYSOS K·B·115 EAA 1926·163

E8 TENEIII TARN -100 DF2 683

E9 FE·I· WURTEMBURG CAF·8

JOGGLES

J1 VINČA II CZÓKA CDP 74 -2300

J2 -700? K·B·110 MYKENAE

J3 -1000 -700 BOLOGNA GREEK M·I·175 K·B·116

J4 -1100 GROTTAFERRATA M·I·136 =NS 1902,167

J5 HERAION ARGOS HOUSE MODEL (WATTLE) MAIA 1923,VII

J6 -600 BOLOGNA M·I·92

J7 -600 BOLOGNA M·I·92

J8 FE·I. VERUCCHIO,FORLI KM

J9 -600 BOLOGNA M·I·92 APULIA vii4 E·APPEN·M·I·159·5

K1 FEI VERUCCHIO FORLI KM

K2 VETULONIA, M·I·200·6

K24 -600 ? TORREGALLI R·M·I·xxxix

K3 FE·I BOLOGNA KM

K4 -700? CUMA MA 1913 XVIII -1100? CAPRI MA 1923 304

K45 CADUA KT40

K5 WURTEMBURG CC·I·25

K9 BR. BEIESK MM·XXX

K6 STYRIA BC·53

K7 -140 NUMANTIA EN·XXXIII

K8 ARDANE CCO·7D

K85 CLONMACNOISE CCO·66

P 1

-550? IALYSOS   SAA·1926·161

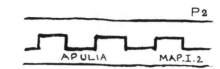

P 2

APULIA   MAP.I.2

P 3

DAUNIA
LATIUM   MAP XIII·7
-700? RHODES   MI·141·14   KB·114

P 4

EM· KALATHIANA, SEAL· EPM·II·26

P 5

PEUKETIA   MAP XXII·10

P 6

HAGENAU   BC·48

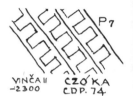

P 7

VINČA II   CZOKA
-2300   CDP·74

P 8

PRE-INCA BOWL
CHIMU PERU

P 9

-700? CRETE   KB·114

V 3

N·APULIA
MAP·XVII·8

V 4

GOTHIC, SWEDEN
AFW 16

V 7

-700?
THERA
KB·114

V 8

+500
RAVENNA
MA·1916 753

V 9

MODERN

FENCE
SZECHUAN
BCA·CXI

W 9

P 92

ANDRONOVO ORAK SIBERIA
STYLE   RV·XIII XCII B

W 1

-1300
IALYSOS
SAA·1926 ƒ80

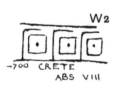

W 2

-700 CRETE
ABS VIII

W 3

BR.
E· APENNINE
MI·130·5

W 4

MID. APULIA
M·AP·XX·8

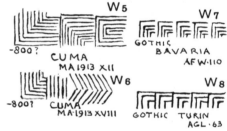

W 5

-800?   CUMA
MA 1913 XII

W 6

-800?   CUMA
MA 1913 XVIII

W 7

GOTHIC
BAVARIA
AFW·110

W 8

GOTHIC TURIN
AGL·63

BARBERINI
MAA 1925 p.62

X 2

-3500   UR

X 3

-3500 UR

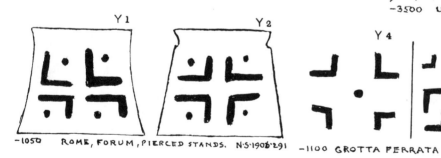

Y 1

Y 2

-1050   ROME, FORUM, PIERCED STANDS.   N·S·1906·291

Y 4

-1100 GROTTA FERRATA

Y 5

NS·1902·185

Y 8

CORNETO   MI·290·2

Y 9

FALERII   MI·320·13

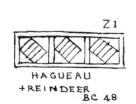

Z 1

HAGUEAU
+REINDEER
BC 48

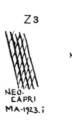

Z 2

LM·III   WT·125
LIANOKLADHI·III

Z 3

NEO.
CAPRI
MA·1923·i

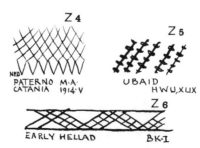

Z 4

NEO.
PATERNO M·A·
CATANIA   1914·V

Z 6

EARLY HELLAD   BK·I

Z 5

UBAID
HWU,XUX

Z 7

BR·AGE RAN98
ROMSDAL

Z 8

-1150
MC 6i6
HUT URN

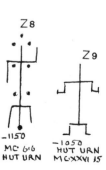

Z 9

-1050
HUT URN
MC·XXVI 15

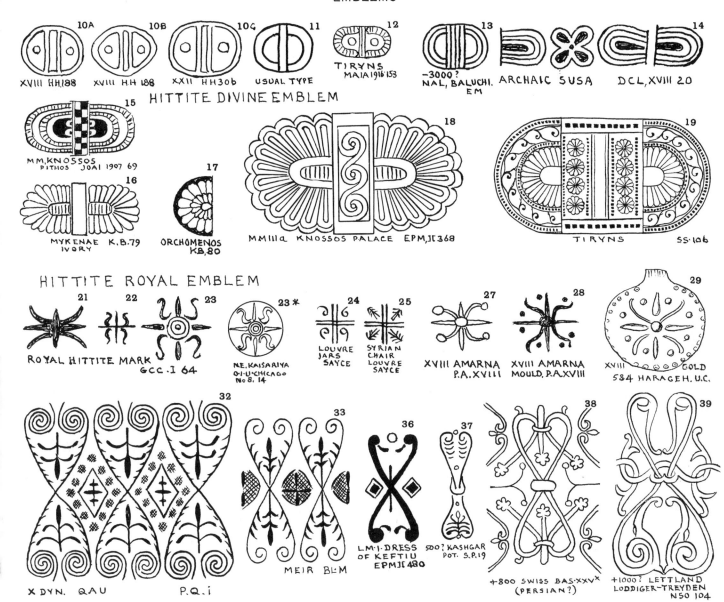

10A XVIII HH.188   10B XVIII HH.188   10C XXII HH30b   11 USUAL TYPE   12 TIRYNS MAIA 1916·153   13 -3000? NAL, BALUCHI. EM   ARCHAIC SUSA   14 DCL. XVIII 20

HITTITE DIVINE EMBLEM

15 MM. KNOSSOS PITHOS JOAI 1907 69   16 MYKENAE K.B.79 IVORY   17 ORCHOMENOS KB.80   18 MMIIIα KNOSSOS PALACE EPM,II 368   19 TIRYNS SS·106

HITTITE ROYAL EMBLEM

21 22 23 ROYAL HITTITE MARK GCC·I 64   23* NE. KAISARIYA O·I·U·CHICAGO No 8, 14   24 LOUVRE JARS SAYCE   25 SYRIAN CHAIR LOUVRE SAYCE   27 XVIII AMARNA P.A. XVIII   28 XVIII AMARNA MOULD, P.A. XVIII   29 XVIII 584 HARAGEH. U.C. GOLD

32 X DYN. QAU   P.Q. i   33 MEIR BL.M   36 LM·I·DRESS OF KEFTIU EPM.II 480   37 500? KASHGAR POT. S.P.19   38 +800 SWISS BAS·XXVˣ (PERSIAN?)   39 +1000? LETTLAND LODDIGER-TREYDEN N50 104

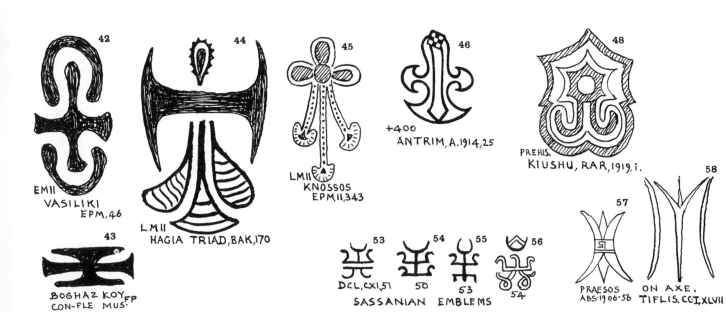

42 EMII VASILIKI EPM, 46   43 BOGHAZ KOY CON-PLE MUS. FP   44 LMII HAGIA TRIAD, BAK, 170   45 LMII KNOSSOS EPM,II,343   46 +400 ANTRIM, A. 1914,25   48 PREHIS. KIUSHU, RAR, 1919, i.

53 DCL, CXI,51   50   54 53   55 53   56 54   SASSANIAN EMBLEMS   57 PRAESOS ABS·1906·56   58 ON AXE, TIFLIS. CCI, XLVII

61 −600? MONTE SANNACE GBA IV.

62 −700? POGGIO SOMMAVILLA NS 1896,479

63 −600? SYRACUSE NS 1895 186

64 −600? MENIDI JI 1899,40

65 +712 S·GIORGIO VALPOLIC⁴ ɸ

66 +712 S·GIORGIO VALPOLICELLA

67 +830 BAGNACAVALLO, FAENZA ɸ

68 +682 S·GIORGIO IN VELABRO FP

69 +825 ɸ ROME S·SABINA

70 FE2 RHEINHESSE DF2 694

71 TENEI. MARNE, DF2, 524

72 MMI·KAMARES MGP. Lxi

73 MMIIA· PALAIKASTRO ABS 1923 SUPR. V

74 MMII, KNOSSOS EPM II IX

75 MM· PHAISTOS·ODEXVI

76 MMIII

77 MMIIIG ZAKRO EPM,II, 125

78 LMI· GOURNIA²HG IX

79 PALAIKASTRO ABS-1903,305

80 SIMILAR BUT CENTRE BHG·⁴L·K

81 +100 ROCKY WOOD HERTS OTP II.12

82 +100 MARTI TOTAVI TIᵢCLAUDIUS PRIMVS ATTII·LIBER ROCKY WOOD HERTS OTP II.12 BMRB 25

83 −480 SCWARTZENBACH BIRKENFELD 25 m E of TREVES. RV·VII·CXCI WITH GQ6,7 LN 71,75

84 +600 KHUSRAU II, ON DRESS. SP.XCIV

85 S·SOFIA SBC XXiv

88 H·SOFIA DECA LXViii

91 −206+25 CHINA S·AᵢC· Viii A

92 +25 TO 220 CHINA SAC.XXII

93 +220 TO 41 CHINA SAC XI

94 +220 TO 41 CHINA SAC XII

95 +227 TO 273 CHINA SAC.XXXIII

97 +25 TO 220 CHINA SAC. XXIII

98 −206+220 CHINA·HSM·9

99 +265 TO 589 CHINA S.A.C. XLIII

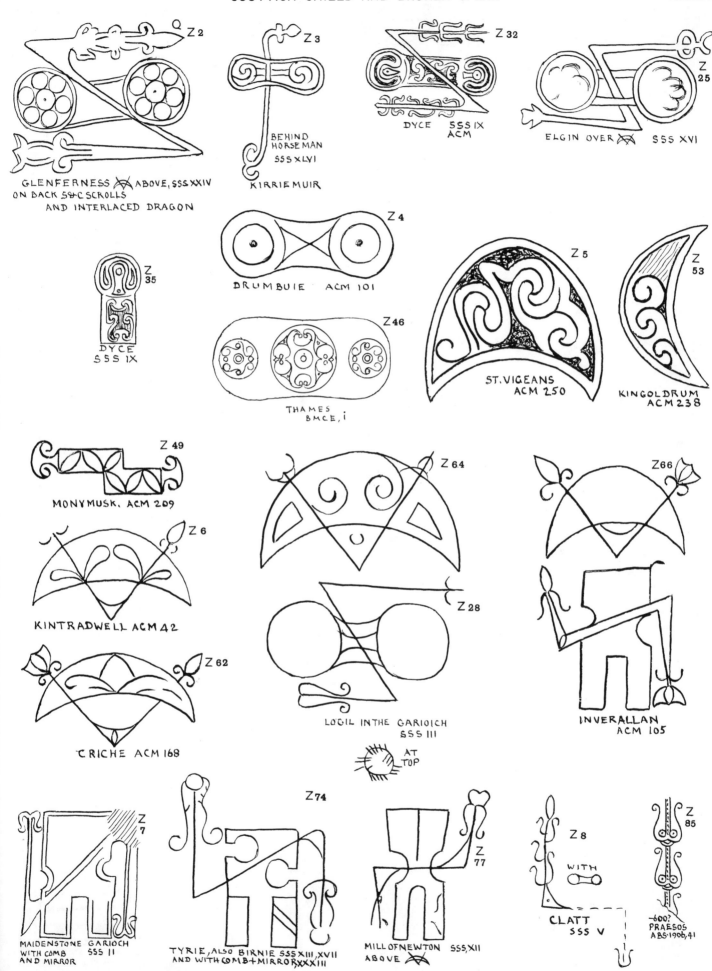

Q Z2
GLENFERNESS ⋈ ABOVE, SSS XXIV
ON BACK S&C SCROLLS
AND INTERLACED DRAGON

Z3
BEHIND
HORSEMAN
SSS XLVI
KIRRIEMUIR

Z 32
DYCE SSS IX
ACM

Z 25
ELGIN OVER ⋈   SSS XVI

Z 35
DYCE
SSS IX

Z 4
DRUMBUIE   ACM 101

Z 46
THAMES
BMCE, i

Z 5
ST. VIGEANS
ACM 250

Z 53
KINGOLDRUM
ACM 238

Z 49
MONYMUSK, ACM 209

Z 6
KINTRADWELL ACM 42

Z 62
CRICHE ACM 168

Z 64

Z 28

LOGIL IN THE GARIOCH
SSS III

AT TOP

Z 66

INVERALLAN
ACM 105

Z 7
MAIDENSTONE GARIOCH
WITH COMB   SSS II
AND MIRROR

Z 74
TYRIE, ALSO BIRNIE SSS XIII, XVII
AND WITH COMB + MIRROR XXXIII

Z 77
MILL OF NEWTON   SSS, XII
ABOVE ⋈

Z 8
WITH
CLATT
SSS V

Z 85
~600?
PRAESOS
ABS 1906, 41

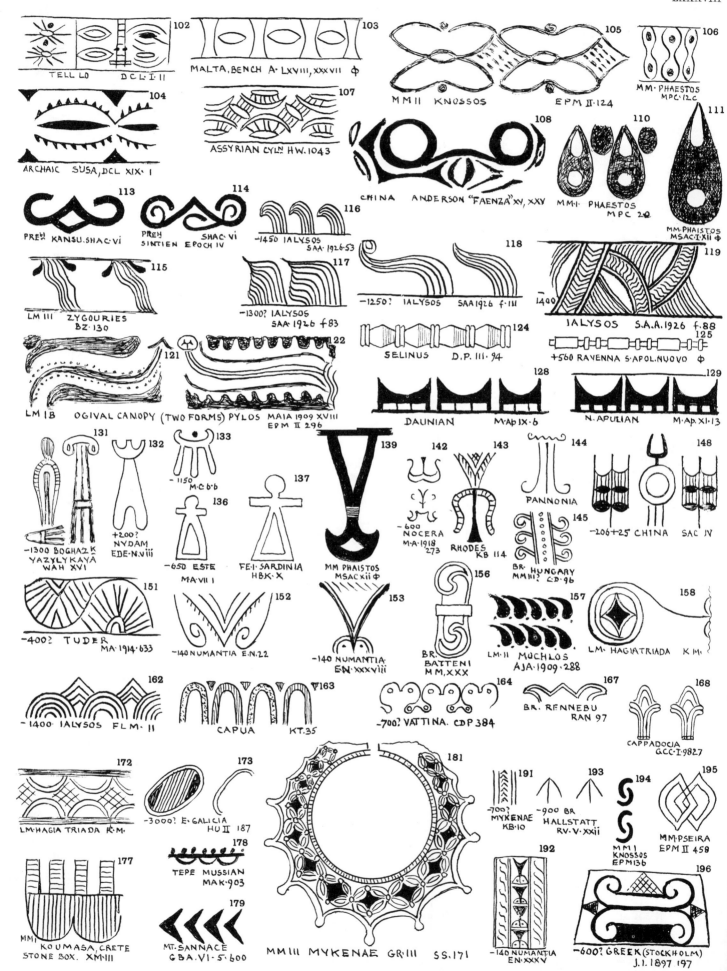

102 TELL LO   DCL·I·11

103 MALTA, BENCH A·LXVIII, XXXVII Φ

104 ARCHAIC SUSA, DCL XIX·1

105 MM II KNOSSOS   EPM II·124

106 MM·PHAESTOS MPC·12C

107 ASSYRIAN CYL.N HW·1043

108 CHINA ANDERSON "FAENZA" XV, XXV

110 MM·I PHAESTOS MPC 2Ω

111 MM·PHAISTOS MSAC·I·XII Φ

113 PREH KANSU·SHAC·VI

114 PREH SINTIEN SHAC·VI EPOCH IV

115 LM III ZYGOURIES BZ·130

116 −1450 IALYSOS SAA·1926·53

117 −1300? IALYSOS SAA·1926 f·83

118 −1250? IALYSOS SAA 1926 f·III

119 −1400 IALYSOS S.A.A. 1926 f·88

121 LM IB

122 OGIVAL CANOPY (TWO FORMS) PYLOS MAIA 1909 XVIII EPM II 296

124 SELINUS D.P. III·94

125 +560 RAVENNA S·APOL·NUOVO Φ

128 DAUNIAN M·Ap IX·6

129 N·APULIAN M·Ap·XI·13

131 −1300 BOGHAZ K YAZYLYKAYA WAH XVI

132 +200? NYDAM EDE·N·VIII

133 −1150 M·C·6·6

136 −650 ESTE MA·VII 1

137 FE·I· SARDINIA HBK·X

139 MM PHAISTOS MSAC XII Φ

142 −600 NOCERA M·A·1918 273

143 RHODES KB 114

144 PANNONIA

145 BR·HUNGARY MM II? C·D·96

148 −206+25 CHINA SAC IV

151 −400? TUDER MA·1914·633

152 −140 NUMANTIA E·N·22

153 −140 NUMANTIA E·N·XXXVIII

156 BR·BATTENI MM·XXX

157 LM·II MUCHLOS AJA·1909·288

158 LM·HAGIA TRIADA K·M·

162 −1400 IALYSOS FLM·11

163 CAPUA KT·35

164 −700? VATTINA CDP 384

167 BR·RENNEBU RAN 97

168 CAPPADOCIA GCC·I·9827

172 LM·HAGIA TRIADA K·M·

173 −3000? E·GALICIA HU II 187

177 MM I KOUMASA, CRETE STONE BOX XM·III

178 TEPE MUSSIAN MAK·903

179 MT·SANNACE GBA·VI·5·600

181 MM III MYKENAE GR·III SS·171

191 −700? MYKENAE KB·10

192 −140 NUMANTIA E·N·XXXV

193 −900 BR HALLSTATT RV·V·XXII

194 MM I KNOSSOS EPM 136

195 MM·PSEIRA EPM II 458

196 −600? GREEK (STOCKHOLM) J.I. 1897 197